Leafy Greens

Other Books by Mark Bittman

Leafy Greens

An A-to-Z guide to 30 types of greens plus more than 120 delicious recipes

MARK BITTMAN

author of
How to Cook
Everything

WILEY

John Wiley & Sons, Inc.

For general information on our other products and services, or technical support, please contact our Customer Care Department within the United States at 800–762–2974, outside the United States at 317–572–3993 or fax 317–572–4002.

Wiley publishes in a variety of print and electronic formats and by print-on-demand. Some material included with standard print versions of this book may not be included in e-books or in print-on-demand. If this book refers to media such as a CD or DVD that is not included in the version you purchased, you may download this material at http://booksupport.wiley.com. For more information about Wiley products, visit www.wiley.com.

Library of Congress Cataloging-in-Publication Data is available upon request.

ISBN 978-1-118-09387-0 (pbk); ISBN 978-1-118-09558-4 (ebk); ISBN 978-1-118-09559-1 (ebk)

Manufactured in the United States of America

10 9 8 7 6 5 4 3 2 1

For Kate and Emma,
who are the best

Contents

. . . . . .

Acknowledgments

The way in which one of life's passing interests becomes a passion strikes me as both mysterious and odd. This one started with a few tomato plants grown in a crack in an asphalt backyard in Somerville, Massachusetts. It continued with larger and more ambitious gardens until the summer I realized that it was growing greens, not exotic eggplants and chiles, that gave me the most satisfaction. Meanwhile, of course, I was cooking.

I loved greens, then, before there was a "reason"—the antioxidant reason—to eat them. Their variety of form, texture, and flavor is unsurpassed in the vegetable kingdom. Read on and see.

I had plenty of help in pursuing this venture. For their recipes, their support, their intelligence, and even their love, I want to thank Pam Anderson, Isabel and Eli Baar, Fern Berman, Jack Bishop, Murray and Gertrude Bittman, Ignacio Blanco, Sally Connolly, Cara Da Silva, Johnny Earles, Bobby Flay, Jean-Louis Gerin, Linda Giuca, Betsy Grauer, Andrea Graziosi, Trish Hall, Pamela Hort, Louise Kennedy, Nora Kerr, Chris Kimball, Michael Lomonaco, Stephanie Lyness, Scott Mowbray, Mitch Orfuss, David Paskin, Chris Schlesinger, Arthur Schwartz, Shari Sucheki, Semeon Tsalbins, and Paula Wolfert. For the ample supply of beautiful organic greens to supplement my own garden during this past, rather stressful summer, I owe a debt of gratitude to Dave Forman and Gilda Outremont.

This book would never have been completed were it not for the energy and intelligence of Angela Miller and Justin Schwartz, the comradeship of John Willoughby, and the partnership of Karen Baar, to whom I owe nearly everything.

Woodbridge, CT

Winter Solstice 1994

New Introduction

I came by writing *Leafy Greens* – this happened in the mid-'90s – quite honestly. It was as natural a decision as *Fish* my first book, which – I can say without exaggerating – was fifteen years in the making. *Leafy Greens* took less than a year because I was in steep immersion.

I had happened onto a preferred style of eating, especially in the summer, that went kind of like this: Garden. Go to fish store. Harvest stuff. Sauté in olive oil. Put fish on top. Steam. Eat.

I'd become, if not a good gardener, if not a devoted gardener, a steady gardener, and one who grew enough vegetables so that I could quit my CSA. (I'm proud to say I was a member of New Haven's first CSA, back in the '80s.)

I began life as the most urban of urbanites, in a housing project in Manhattan, and I don't even think I saw a garden up close until I was 20. When I rented my first apartment, for some reason (a reason as inexplicable to me as that which caused me to start cooking), I planted tomato seeds by a fence – in the cracks in the concrete in the backyard (really) – and grew tomatoes. When I bought my first house, part of the appeal was that I could have a garden. And by the late '80s, I was pretty darned avid.

The thing is – and this is consistent with my cooking – I was lazy. I didn't like weeding, messing with chemicals (I became an "organic" gardener not so much out of principle but because I could never be bothered to get out there and spray or dust), tying things up, thinning, or dying crops. I especially did not like dying crops, and so my main plantings were in greens.

Have you ever grown arugula? You put it in the ground, it pops up, two weeks later you can be eating it and replanting it. Lettuce takes a little more time, but not much more care, and you can start giving the little seedlings "haircuts" pretty early in their lives – that's the origin of real mesclun mixes. Kale and collards – so great – can be planted early, grown quite late (reliably through Thanksgiving in Connecticut), and are impossible to kill. And so on.

Thus *Leafy Greens* was written by a gardener. Now, however – living once again in the city – a garden is out of my reach. Fortunately the greens themselves are everywhere. (Although the arugula and mesclun you buy in stores is a pale shadow of those you grow yourself, as gardeners know.) Not much else has changed. Greens are good for you; greens are delicious; greens are inexpensive and abundant and earth-friendly and kind to animals.

There's not much I'd change about this book; it represents a moment in time, and I'm flattered that both readers and publishers believe that it deserves to be reprinted. I could tinker with a recipe here and there, but I've come to see most of these as old friends. I'll rewrite the whole thing in ten years, when I'm back to living in a place with a garden. Inshallah.

Mark Bittman

New York City, summer 2011

introduction

● ● ● ● ●

IT'S NO SECRET that vegetables, grains, and fruits are the future of the American diet; recent statistics show that health-conscious people are eating less meat and that this practice is becoming a habit. Many people, however, are looking to get past what has become a pasta-dominated way of eating.

Looking back over the past few years, it's clear that we emerged from the '80s craving the strong flavors we grew to love as the new American cuisine developed. But as we turned from red meats to chicken, grains, and legumes, we found that because these foods are essentially bland, it takes more work to make them taste good (few foods pack as much flavor with as little work as a grilled steak). I remember an article I wrote about chicken for *Cook's* in 1990, the thrust of which was that since we were now eating less bold-flavored foods, we were going to have to learn how to cook them with flavorful sauces, using the herbs, spices, and flavors of the international community. That is exactly what has happened.

Leafy greens, however, don't require that kind of flavor-building workup because they contain as much intrinsic taste as any other food group on earth (which undoubtedly explains why most kids find them fearsome).

Still, greens have taken some getting used to. When I was a child, iceberg lettuce was the only fresh green that regularly appeared in our house—cabbage never showed its head, collards were as likely to grace the table as was milkweed, dandelions were for blowing, and spinach was inevitably canned.

But the past 30 years have seen a convergence of factors that have boosted the green vegetable to prominence.

- Superior transportation and new hybrids made fresh vegetables a staple throughout the country, even in winter.
- We have developed a cuisine of shared cultures, which means that dandelions, for example, are no longer the exclusive property of Italians.
- We always knew that vegetables were good for us, but we didn't know how good. (Nor did we know how bad for us some of the alternatives are.)
- Finally, we learned how to cook. Although Italian cooking teacher and author Giuliano Bugialli has remarked, "We Italians do not undercook our vegetables," we Americans have learned that while some vegetables respond well to long, slow cooking, others can be quick-steamed or sautéed with crunchy and delicious results.

The upshot of all this is that there are more green, leafy vegetables in our markets than we've ever seen before, begging to be tossed in salads, stir-fried, sautéed, and stewed. And, unlike beans and even some meats, each is distinctive. In fact, it would be easier to determine the difference in the dark between steamed, unadorned collards and dandelions and steamed—or even sautéed—veal and chicken.

When I say "leafy greens," I'm talking about everything from spinach and chard to dandelions, kale, turnip greens, lettuces, watercress, and more. (In my garden every year we grow at least twenty different greens, not including lettuces.) Lettuces are a part of this mix, too, and although they don't pack the nutritional or flavor punch of the darker greens, lettuces are interesting thanks to their sheer variety—these days, you can find at least a half-dozen varieties even in supermarkets, and the selection in specialty stores (and in California markets) is stunning.

The sheer number of edible greens—probably about 300 in this country alone—means that I've had to make some choices about what not to cover in these pages. Basically, I've eliminated the most esoteric greens, those available only to gardeners (at this date; this will change), wild greens that are never (again, subject to change) sold in stores—such as nettles and milkweed—herbs that are sometimes used as greens, like parsley and burnet, and the greens of flowers, many of which are good to eat. What I have included are all the good eating greens that you are likely to find in specialty stores, farmers' markets, and of course supermarkets. Which still leaves us with several dozen in this book.

When they are extremely young, any greens—from Chinese cabbages such as bok choi to dark greens like kale or watercress—make delicious additions to green salads; mixed with lettuces, herbs, and even flowers, they form the wonderful mixed-salad combination known in southern France (and, often, in this country) as "mesclun." Although greens are beginning to appear with some regularity in specialty food stores and even supermarkets, gardeners are most likely to take advantage of them in this way. (Gardeners should see "A Note to the Gardener," page 187.)

As they grow larger, however, most greens become bitter in their raw state; they also become tougher with age. Never fear: Cooking techniques for all of them are quick and simple. Almost any green can be sautéed or used in stir-fries, or stewed to a melting tenderness. There is nothing easier than cooking greens, and few things more rewarding.

Eating Greens for Health

For me, flavor is enough of a reason to eat leafy greens; but the fact that they are arguably the most valuable foodstuffs on the planet doesn't hurt.

Although the National Cancer Institute's effort urging us to eat five fruits and vegetables a day is sound—whenever any plant food replaces a cheeseburger, a bag of chips, or a bowl of ice cream, your intake of total fat, saturated fat, and calories is likely to decrease, and with it your risk of most chronic diseases—the nutritional content of most vegetables simply clobbers that of most fruits. Although grapes, for example, contain some fiber and a smattering of vitamin C, collards are so packed with nutrients that if they were a manufactured food, the FDA might insist that they undergo tests. From a nutritional perspective, dark green leafy vegetables are the superstars of the food world.

Most dark greens are high in traditional nutrients such as vitamins C and E and beta carotene, powerful antioxidants whose cancer-fighting role is only just being appreciated; folic acid, recently found to play a part in preventing neural tube birth defects and also possibly a major contributor to the fight against cancer (research is in the early stages); and tumor-reducing fiber. Some also contain significant amounts of iron and calcium (of special importance to vegetarians) as well as important trace elements from the soil such as magnesium, zinc, selenium, manganese, and copper.

In addition, there is the almost staggering list of micro-, or nontraditional nutrients, whose names are unknown to those outside of the nutrition field: lutein, dithiolthiones, glucosinolates and indoles, isothiocyanates and thiocyanates, and more. These are found in most green leafy vegetables and are now believed to be the equal of beta carotene when it comes to preventing cancer; some reduce tumor production and growth, others combat hormone-related cancers, still others cleanse the system by inducing the body's own production of enzymes that in turn flush carcinogens from the system. Some of these nutrients are also thought to prevent heart disease.

Which of these compounds are most important? Which greens contain the most and offer the most benefit? How many servings of greens should you eat? These are the questions that many researchers are focusing on. For now, however, no one knows how much of each nutrient is in each green, and that information, expensive and time consuming to obtain, may not be immediately forthcoming.

In any case, we do know that all greens are abundant in important nutrients, and that's good enough for me.

Cooking Greens for Maximum Nutrition

Getting people to eat dark green leafy vegetables, which should be an easy task, has been largely confounded by the myth that greens lose their nutrients if you cook them for more than a minute or two. The essential problem is that if older broccoli raab, collards, or mustard greens are not cooked long enough, you end up chewing on woody stalks.

Yet although undercooked greens may contain more nutrients than those cooked to tenderness, thorough cooking is far from criminal. In fact, there is no canon when it comes to cooking greens, at least from a nutritional perspective; they are so varied that one method or another is always appropriate. Young dandelions or mustard greens, even very young kale can be eaten raw in a salad (and, in fact, are often part of the mesclun mix served in restaurants and now sold in many stores). Older, tougher greens—whose stems are a 1/4 inch or so at their widest point—should be simmered until tender, then drained and served or sautéed for extra flavor. Mature but still relatively tender greens can be sautéed directly, or briefly steamed; chop them up while raw to further reduce cooking time and make serving easier.

What is true is that boiling vegetables to death destroys many valuable nutrients. But how much cooking is needed, and what kind is best? Generally, cooking increases bioavailability of some nutrients but destroys others. Nutrients are lost in two ways: Those that are water soluble such as vitamin C, the B vitamins, and many minerals, are often poured down the drain; up to 50 percent of the vitamin C content of most vegetables, for example, is lost in the cooking water. These and many others can be destroyed by excessive heat.

The answer is to cook vegetables long enough to open the pores of the food system, the fibrous matrix surrounding nutrients, but not so long as to destroy those nutrients; and use as little water as possible. In short, you want to sauté, stir-fry, parboil, steam, or microwave vegetables until they are just al dente, fairly tender but retaining a bit of crunch.

How to Buy, Store, Wash, and Dry Greens

There was a time when every story about vegetables included a section that began "Look for firm, unbruised leaves…" That about sums up what you need to know to buy greens; it's all quite obvious. Buy the best-looking greens you can find: without brown spots, bashed-in parts, chewed-up leaves; nothing dried out, moldy, slimy, and so on.

Greens will wilt once they're out of the ground and away from moisture; that's why supermarkets have installed elaborate spraying systems. Unless you intend to install a similar device in your home refrigerator, I recommend that you put your greens in plastic bags when you get home; you can wash them first if you like, but make sure they're not too wet—if too much moisture gets sealed inside the bags, the leaves will start to rot. Needless to say, it's best to cook greens sooner rather than later, but it's also safe to assume that they will retain their quality for a few days in your refrigerator.

For some reason, washing and drying greens presents an enormous challenge to many people (including those who work in restaurants; that's why we've all eaten so much sandy spinach). Done correctly, however, this is about as simple a kitchen task as there is. And the technique remains the same regardless of the greens you are cleaning; the only differences occur with really large bunches of greens, like collards, which are best chopped up first for easier handling, and with those greens that will be used in salads, which must be dried after washing.

Here are the steps for washing:

1. Fill a large pot, the bottom portion of a salad spinner, or an entire sink, with cold water.
2. Put the greens in a strainer, a colander, or the colander-like portion of a salad spinner.
3. Plunge that colander into the water and swish the greens around. Remove the colander.
4. Look at the water. Does it have sand in it? Drain it, rinse the pot or sink, and repeat the process until the water is clean.

That's it. If you're making salad, you really should dry the greens also, for two reasons: One, water that clings to the leaves will cause any oily dressing to slide right off, and two, that same water will dilute your brilliant dressing.

Salad spinners do a great job of drying greens; if you're more compulsive than me, you might roll them up in paper or cloth towels after spinning them to get them extra dry. However, a little moisture doesn't seem to make much difference.

When you're stuck without a salad spinner (hey—these things happen), resort to the two-step method. First, leave the greens to sit in a colander for a half hour or so; much of the moisture will drain away naturally (if the weather is really hot, do this in the refrigerator). Then go get a clean pillowcase, put the greens therein, go out onto the porch, fire escape, deck, sidewalk, terrace, balcony, or what have you, and swing that pillowcase around so that the centrifugal force forces the water from the greens, through the linen, and into the air. (This is what you call fun.) If you don't have a pillowcase, use a sheet or a thin towel or your shirt—almost anything will work.

How to Prepare and Cook Greens

There are greens that cook almost instantly, like spinach, and those that take some time, like kale. But all greens have a couple of things in common. They must be washed before cooking (page 6 and above), and some judgment must be made about the stems.

My general rule is that a stem less than an eighth of an inch thick can be pretty much treated the same as the leaves; cooking time will have to be adjusted upward, but only slightly. With larger but not enormous stems—say, those between an eighth and a quarter of an inch—I usually strip the leaves, chop the stems, and begin cooking them first, adding the leaves only after the stems have begun to become tender. Thicker stems should be peeled, cooked separately, cooked for much longer than the greens or—in the case of slow-cooked collards, for example—the whole mess of greens and stems cooked for so long that it no longer matters.

You can sidestep this whole issue by discarding stems, but I don't recommend that. First of all, you paid for them (and, by weight and bulk, they often make up more of the plant than the leaves). Second, there's work involved in this, too, because it makes your initial cleaning more cumbersome. Finally, there's no reason not to eat stems; they're good.

So, with greens such as spinach, I pick off the largest stems, especially if they've begun to brown on the ends (as they so often have). With most other greens, from dandelion and arugula to kale and mustard, I just take a knife and chop off the last half inch or so of stems, where they have dried out. With thick-stemmed collards, kale, and the like, I occasionally separate stems and leaves but always cook both, peeling if necessary, as described above. With chard, which is a special case, I occasionally use the stems and leaves in different dishes.

When it comes to cooking, you have to make decisions case by case. You can steam most greens. I find steaming imprecise, however, and have burned both pot and green more times than I can count, especially when I have tried to steam greens such as kale, which can take fifteen minutes or more. Still, steaming is quick (you don't have to bring a large pot of water to a boil) and easy: Put a half inch or so of water in a pot you can cover, put the greens on a rack or even a plate above the water, cover, and turn on the heat. Check often so you'll know when the greens are done (and to avoid burning the pot).

After years and years of experimentation, though, I have come to prefer the time-honored method of parboiling my greens for most uses. Here's how I cook spinach now, for example: I bring a large pot of water to a boil, salt it, plunge in my washed spinach, push it under the surface with a big spoon, and remove it immediately. Elapsed cooking time: 30 seconds. Number of ruined servings of spinach: 0. Number of burnt pots: 0. The only downside is that you must remember, in advance, to set that pot of water to boil. (I often wind up using that same pot of water for pasta; after I remove the greens with a skimmer, tongs, or slotted spoon, I cook the pasta in the same water.)

This not-especially revolutionary method works perfectly in most circumstances. You don't need to cover the pot, so it's easy to keep an eye on progress and to stop the cooking at any moment. Keep a colander in a bowl of ice water in the sink and plunge the greens into that when they are just where you want them. This method preserves color beautifully.

I cook greens this way whether I want to serve them hot, in which case I just drain and dress them; or cold, in which case I plunge them into my ice water, wait a minute or two, and squeeze dry before refrigerating or dressing and serving.

I also cook greens this way if I want to finish them by another cooking method, such as sautéing or stir-frying. This is especially useful if the greens are not tender enough for direct sautéing or stir-frying, as is often the case with kale, bok choi, collards, broccoli raab, mustard, and other like greens. In this case, I put the greens into the boiling water, cook them until they are nearly but not quite tender, then plunge them into my ice water. When they're cool enough to handle, I squeeze out the liquid, chop them up, and add them, at the appropriate time, to my stir-fry or sauté. You'll find dozens of recipes using this technique in this book.

A word about microwaving: I occasionally microwave greens but only if the quantity is small. Although there have been improvements in microwave technology, it still cooks foods unevenly, and it still takes quite a while when quantities increase past a serving or two. Microwave if you will, adding a small amount of water, along with the greens, to a covered microwave container, and cook at two-minute intervals, checking and stirring frequently.

The Greens

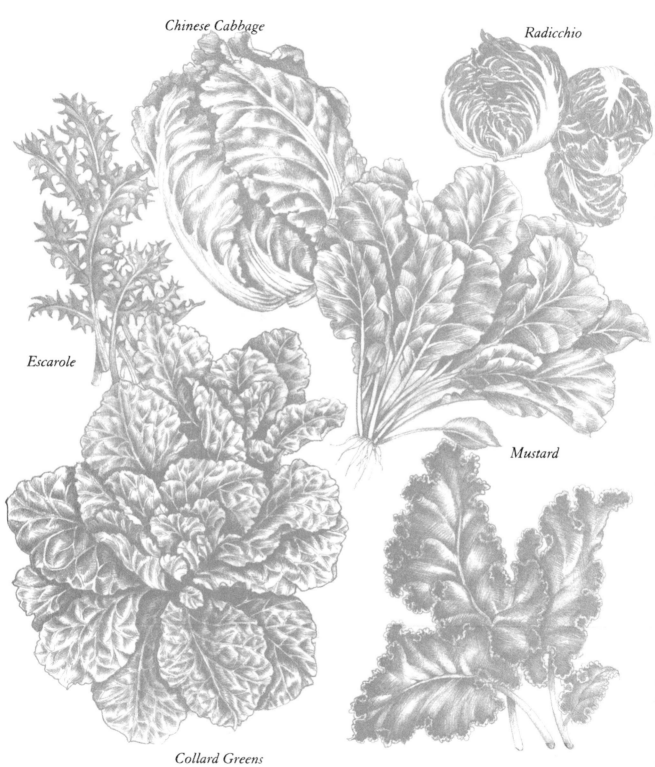

Chinese Cabbage

Radicchio

Escarole

Mustard

Collard Greens

Kale

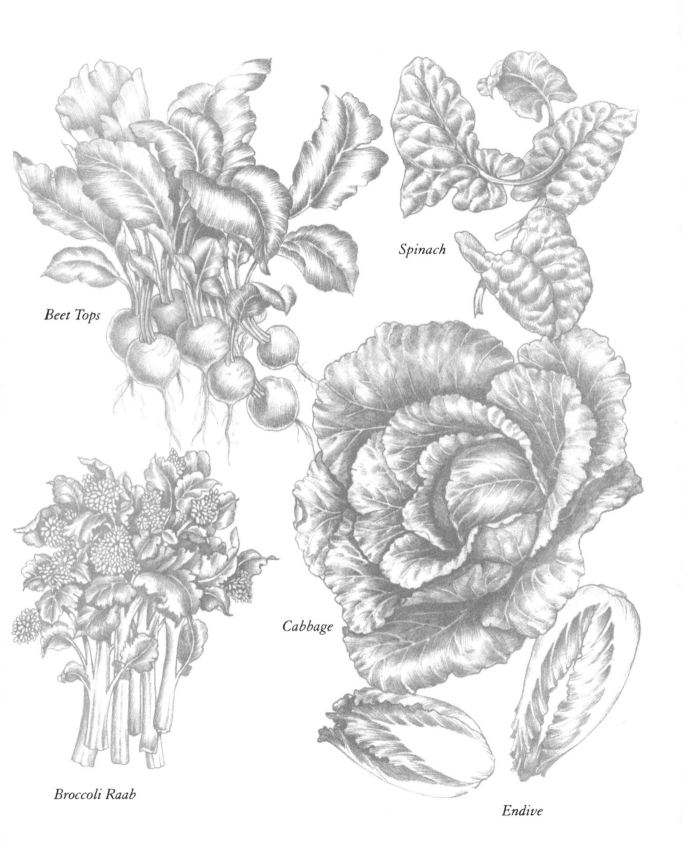

Spinach

Beet Tops

Cabbage

Broccoli Raab

Endive

Alaria

See Sea vegetables, pages 34-36.

Amaranth (pigweed, tumbleweed, amaranth spinach, Chinese spinach, hin choy)

Amaranthus hybridus var. erythrostachyus

Varieties: There are a few available to the gardener, mostly grown for flowers; to my knowledge, no amaranth is grown commercially for its greens (some is grown for its highly nutritious seed, which is so tiny it takes 700,000 to make a pound). If you're going to grow amaranth, try Red Stripe or any other variety with variegated leaves and the signature red seed plume.

Buying: You won't be able to.

Nutritional Information: Good source of calcium and other minerals; decent source of antioxidants, especially beta-carotene.

To Cook: Treat as spinach. Leave all but the thickest stems on. Good in stir-fries.

Substitutes: Spinach.

Arame

See Sea vegetables, pages 34-36.

$\mathcal{A}$rugula (roquette, rocket, Italian cress)

Eruca vesicaria, eruca sativa

Varieties: There are other salad greens known as rocket, wall rocket *(Diplotaxis muralis)* and sea rocket *(Cakile maritima)*. They bear a vague resemblance in flavor and appearance to arugula but are rarely seen outside the Mediterranean.

Buying: Look for fresh, shiny dark green leaves, about two to four inches long.

Nutritional Information: Exceptionally high in beta carotene, vitamin C, and calcium; decent source of iron.

To Cook: Traditionally, arugula is used almost exclusively as a salad green. I like it stir-fried as well, and many chefs like to use it as a base for grilled or sautéed meats or fish, which wilts the green when placed on top. An all-arugula salad is a treat as long as the greens are young, but they are too hot for most people when they become older, at which point they should be mixed with other greens.

Substitutes: Watercress and dandelion are both peppery, strong-tasting salad greens that can be substituted for arugula; all three have distinct flavors that would not be confused with one another.

Arugula has dark green, lobed leaves that resemble oak leaves. Popular in Italy and southern France, arugula is an essential ingredient of the salad mix known as mesclun (page 30) and makes a terrific salad on its own.

When I first tasted this strong, distinctly flavored green, about 20 years ago, I found it unpalatable. I would have described its taste as that of spicy mud; now, I can scarcely go without that tangy, peppery flavor. (Was my first arugula overpowering or did I become accustomed to its charms? I'll never know.)

Arugula is a favorite of gardeners because it is easy to grow and fast—you can begin harvesting just weeks after planting, when the leaves are a couple of inches high. (In fact, I could never figure out if arugula was also called rocket because of its fast growth or assertive flavor.) Because arugula can withstand several degrees of frost, you can begin sowing seed in very early spring and continue right into fall. This procedure will insure a constant supply of fresh young leaves, important because mature plants can become unpleasantly hot, and arugula quickly goes to seed in midsummer.

Beet Greens

See Swiss chard.

Belgian endive (chicory, witloof, endive, chicon, radicchio)

Cichorium intybus

Varieties: There are many chicories, white, green, and red; they are often confused with their close relatives, the endives and escaroles (pages 24-25). One of the chicories is the witloof, which Americans know as Belgian endive and the French call endive. Witloof is the blanched leaves of the plant, grown in darkness to keep it mild and white; it is all that is considered here (information about other chicories, endives, and escaroles can be found under those headings).

It's all very confusing, of course, and attempts to straighten this out have failed. Probably the best thing to do is to continue to use the term *Belgian endive* for the blanched root and the words *chicory, endive, escarole,* and *radicchio* for everything else. That's what I have chosen to do.

Buying: Since all chicories, including Belgian endive, are crops of the late fall and winter, many are available when other interesting salad greens are scarce.

When buying Belgian endive, look for leaves with a yellow rather than a green tip; the whiter the better. They are sometimes wrapped in paper to keep them from the light, which turns them green and bitter.

Nutritional Information: Belgian endive is not a nutritional powerhouse; it's got a bit of calcium and some iron.

To Cook: Belgian endive is typically bittersweet but not bitter, and very crunchy. The leaves are small, pointy, and somewhat cup shaped, so they lend themselves to fillings. Cut across their length, they form perfect little rings that give salads a bit more visual appeal. Belgian endive is also good braised.

Substitutes: There is no substitute for Belgian endive.

Belgian endives are expensive little devils, four to six inches long. They grow from the root of the chicory plant (which explains all the confusion detailed above), which is first cultivated outside, then cut back to within an inch of the crown; the roots are then transplanted into a box filled with soil and covered with several inches of sand, sawdust, or similar material. The roots are kept dark, cool (about 50 degrees), and moist; a month or so later, the crowns have resprouted and produced the familiar white heads. Should you try this operation yourself (I did, and it was rewarding enough, although not something I'd choose to do regularly), cut off those heads and let the roots produce another.

Bok Choi

See Chinese cabbage, pages 21-22.

Broccoli Raab

(rape, rabe, cima di rape, rapini, ruvo kale, flowering cabbage)

Brassica campestris var. napus or *B. rapa*

Varieties: There is only one true broccoli raab, and you're unlikely to encounter anything else by this name; one of the flowering Chinese cabbages is close in appearance but usually has paler stems.

Buying: Look for firm green leaves and flower heads that are developed but not yet open or showing more than a tiny hint of yellow. Thinner stems are better—they will cook more quickly, require no peeling, and be more tender.

Nutritional Information: Good source of beta carotene and iron; very good source of vitamin C and calcium.

To Cook: Assuming you like bitter foods, you'll find the leaves, stems, and flowers of broccoli raab all edible and delicious. Before cooking, remove any wilted or yellowed leaves; peel or discard those stems more than half an inch thick. Broccoli raab can be steamed, sautéed, parboiled, even baked.

Substitutes: Mustard and turnip greens are close in flavor and nutritional content. Because they have thinner stems and are rarely sold in flower, the texture is quite different.

Broccoli raab, a traditional Italian vegetable, is the flowering stalk and leaves of a member of the *brassica* family, which includes not only broccoli but also cabbage, mustard, and turnip. Its small broccoli-like florets taste like broccoli, although they are more bitter, and the mustard-like greens pack a bit of a punch. Young broccoli raab, available mostly to gardeners, is excellent raw in salads; most broccoli raab is served cooked. Like many other greens, broccoli raab will tolerate light frost, so it can be sown very early in spring and harvested late into the fall.

Cabbage (see also Chinese cabbage)

Brassica oleracea capatata (green or red)

Varieties: The most important other variety of heading cabbage is the Savoy *(B. oleracea sabauda),* which is also known as Milan cabbage. Gardeners have access to dozens, even hundreds, of varieties of heading cabbages, but almost all are variations on the common green or red or Savoy.

Buying: Cabbage matures late and stores well, making it a good winter green. Common cabbage, whether green or red, should be firm, with smooth, brightly colored and unblemished outer leaves; it should feel heavy. Savoy cabbage is lighter and has rough, crinkled leaves.

Nutritional Information: The more we find out about cabbage and its relatives—the dark greens, broccoli, and so on—the more important they seem to be. They are decent sources of carotenes, potassium, calcium, and folic acid, and very good sources of vitamin C and fiber. Cabbages, like the dark leafy greens, are being vigorously studied for their cancer-fighting potential.

To Cook: Because it is sweet and crunchy, cabbage is delicious raw and is good shredded and added to salads (red cabbage, of course, is especially striking). Cabbage can be cooked in many ways—braised, sautéed, stewed, stir-fried, or pickled, as in sauerkraut. When cooking red cabbage, add a bit of vinegar or lemon juice to the liquid to keep the cabbage a bright color.

Substitutes: Some Chinese cabbages (especially Napa) are similar in texture and flavor.

Common green or red cabbage is characterized by a compact head formed by its leaves, although the head may be conical, round, or on the flat side; Savoy cabbage, with its crinkly leaves, is especially delicious, and given a choice, I'd always go for the Savoy.

Cabbage is one of our oldest known and earliest cultivated greens; there are records of it being cooked 4,000 years ago. Its health benefits have been hinted at since at least the time of Pliny, but so have its drawbacks: It can smell up a house if it is overcooked and become a soggy mess if it is cooked too long in too much water.

Nevertheless, cabbage is fabulous as long as it is treated properly, which to me at least means cooking with a minimum of liquid; or in a soup (except for, of course, corned beef and cabbage, in which a bit of a soggy mess is part of the tradition).

Cabbage is also quite easy to grow (like most greens) and produces large quantities of dense food with little work. Which brings me to sauerkraut, a not quite universally loved concoction that is nothing more than cabbage pickled in salt. You can make your own sauerkraut, and it isn't difficult, but it is time- and space-consuming, and few persons bother.

Buying it is much more common; I recommend doing so at a health food store, where no-chemical kraut is sold—you don't need preservatives in sauerkraut (or any other pickle, for that matter; that's why pickles exist in the first place!).

Chicory (endive, escarole, radicchio; see also endive, Belgian endive, escarole)

Chicorium intybus

This is the same plant responsible for producing Belgian endive, but here we'll consider the leafy chicories, of which there are green and red varieties; the most beautiful of the latter group is what we call radicchio (the Italians call all chicories "radicchio"). Some of the more popular green varieties are Sugar Loaf and Grumulo. Of the red, Red Verona, Variegated Castelfranco, and Red Treviso (really *rosso di Treviso*) are tried and true.

> Buying: Chicories can form tight or loose heads; just make sure leaves are plump rather than dried out.
>
> Nutritional Information: Chicories offer good amounts of calcium and iron, along with decent amounts of vitamin C and loads of beta carotene.
>
> To Cook: Most chicories are served in mixed salads (they're generally considered too bitter to serve without milder greens), and the red ones are especially attractive. Radicchios are also good baked, roasted, grilled, and braised.
>
> Substitutes: In salads, chicories, endives, escarole, radicchio, and dandelion can be used interchangeably. For cooking, radicchio is best.

Wild chicory is the tall gray-green leafed plant with blue, dandelion-like flowers that is often found along roadsides; like many lettuces, this omnipresent weed belongs to the daisy family. Wild chicory can be eaten, although it is quite bitter unless it is picked in early spring. Get as much of the white crown as you can, and use it, with the greens, as a salad herb, much like dandelion. You also can cook the whole plant top as a potherb, seasoning with butter and salt. Its roots can be roasted and used as a coffee substitute.

Other chicories have been cultivated from this plant, and now there are an incredible and rather confusing variety. In Italy, where chicories are often named after their region (*rosso di Treviso*), they are often sold with a piece of the root, which is peeled and eaten; it is exceptionally crisp. In this country, we see radicchio and the kinds of chicory called endive or escarole.

If you grow chicory, sow seeds in midsummer for a fall or winter crop; the plants can also be wintered for spring green. Bear in mind that the red varieties start out green; their color changes when the cooler night temperatures of autumn arrive. The young leaves are quite mild and become increasingly bitter with age. Light frosts tame the flavor somewhat.

Chinese cabbage (bok choi, Napa, nappa, pe-tsai, celery cabbage, Michihili cabbage, tatsoi, tientsin, Chinese oil vegetable, Chinese broccoli, Peking cabbage, Shanghai cabbage, etc.)

Brassica rapa, pekinensis group (elongated head such as Napa)

Brassica rapa, chinensis group (chardlike such as bok choi)

Brassica chinensis (flat, dark green, glossy leaves such as tatsoi)

Varieties: Endless, as you can see. Supermarkets usually carry bok choi and Napa; tatsoi is becoming popular as a salad green but so far only in mesclun mixes; you can find almost any of the other varieties from time to time in Asian markets.

Buying: Heading cabbages such as Napa should be tight and heavy; bok choi and other thick-stemmed cabbages should be unbruised and fleshy.

Nutritional Information: High in beta carotene, vitamin C, potassium, some B vitamins, and fiber.

To Cook: Heading cabbages can be treated much like green or red cabbage; bok choi can be used like chard. All Chinese cabbages are good in stir-fries and soups; braised, with or without meat; pickled (as in kimchee). Young Chinese cabbages, or the tatsoi variety, are excellent in salads.

Substitutes: For bok choi, chard, which is close enough for most purposes; for the heading cabbages, common head cabbage; for tatsoi, young mustard, arugula, or cress.

Among Chinese cabbages, the bok choi varieties really stand apart; their texture can be as crunchy as that of celery if cooking times are short, but if you leave them in the pan a little longer, they develop a creamy texture that is unique among greens. For my money, their flavor is superior to that of any other cabbage.

Collards

Brassica oleracea, Acephala group

Buying: Look for dark green color and firm unwilted leaves. Young leaves with stems no thicker than a pencil will be easier to clean, less wasteful, cook more quickly, and have a better texture when cooked.

Nutritional Information: Collards are a decent source of iron, calcium, magnesium, potassium, and phosphorus as well as many of the B vitamins, vitamins A, C, E, and K; they're a good source of beta carotene as well.

To Cook: Remove any thick tough stems, or peel them (a thankless task). As with other tough dark greens, you can steam them (which preserves a few more nutrients) or boil them (which does a better job of preserving color) or stir-fry them with a bit of water or stock; most collards are too tough to stir-fry without liquid. If, however, you grow collards, you can harvest the tender leaves at the top of the plant and stir-fry them or use the youngest thinnings in salads.

The large, almost leathery leaves of collards are a beautiful dark green color. They have long been a favorite in the South, partly because of their heat tolerance, but like the kale to which they are intimately related, collards are at their sweetest when grown in cool weather. In fact, collards are known for their hardiness and can be harvested even in the snow.

Dandelion (pissenlit, cow-parsnip)

Taraxacum officinale

Varieties: In Europe dandelions are so popular that the European farmers cultivate several varieties—those with big crowns, with thicker leaves, and so on. But for our purposes, dandelions are either wild or store-bought.

Buying: The most important thing you need to know about dandelions is, the smaller the better. Leaves longer than six inches are almost certainly too bitter to eat raw. If you can get part of the crown—the white part at the base of the leaves—so much the better.

Nutritional Information: Dandelions are among the most nutritious foods known, containing more protein, fiber, calcium, and potassium than any other green. They're so loaded with beta carotene that one half expects them to be regulated by the Food and Drug Administration.

To Cook: Leaves can be sandy; wash them well. Use young greens in a salad with olive oil and salt, and to counteract bitterness, add slightly more vinegar or lemon juice than you would on an ordinary salad. Older greens taste better steamed or sautéed like spinach.

Substitutes: Wild chicory is very close; in salads, any of the nonheading chicories, endive, escarole, or radicchio, will provide similar flavor.

Dandelion leaves, which can grow up to 10 inches long, are deeply toothed (the name mean's "lion's tooth") with a white midrib; the plant forms a rosette at its base. If you grow dandelions, or want to take advantage of the wild ones growing near your house, try hiding the foliage from the sun (using boards or earth) when they are about three-quarters grown; they will turn white and taste less bitter. If you're picking wild dandelions, pick them as early as possible in the spring and of course from a place where no sprays have been used.

Dandelion greens have long been used by the French and Italians as a spring tonic for the blood after a long winter and by herbalists as a reliable diuretic (the French name *pissenlit* alludes to this, not too indirectly). Now, one of the surest signs of spring is the appearance of the dandelion in supermarkets; they are cheap, plentiful, and easy to grow. With luck, they will be native to your area and reasonably fresh.

Dulse

See Sea vegetables, pages 34-36.

Endive (curly endive, frisee)

Cichorium endivia var. crispa

See escarole; this is another variation of the same species, with finely cut, narrow, twisted curly leaves; it appears to be frilly. Its outer leaves are dark green, fading to a lighter lemony color on the interior. Other than for appearance the two are identical.

Escarole (Scarole, Batavia, Batavian endive)

Cichorium endivia var. latifolia

Varieties: There are many, but they are primarily of interest to gardeners; we have grown and enjoyed "Cuore Pieno," an escarole with pretty yellow inner leaves; and "Nuvol," which has an especially sweet heart.

Buying: Leaves should be somewhat fleshy, thicker than those of lettuce. Heads should be loose and shaggy but have a well-defined heart.

Nutritional Information: Strong in the calcium department, only moderate amounts of the antioxidants.

To Cook: Wash well; there may be sand. Use as an addition to salads. Fabulous in soups, with beans, braised with loads of garlic and olive oil.

Substitutes: Any of the endives or chicories, especially curly endive.

Escarole, another of the endive-chicory clan, is a lettuce-like salad green, especially favored in France and Italy, with a somewhat nutty but bitter flavor.

In hot weather this bitter flavor becomes pronounced and escarole goes to seed, so if you are growing it, harvest in early spring and replant for a fall harvest, or give it some shade during the summer. Gardeners and those near a good farmers' market have a real advantage, with access to varieties that are crunchy and mild, unlike the tough and sometimes bitter greens available at the supermarket.

Hiziki

See Sea vegetables, pages 34-36.

Kale

Brassica Oleracea acephala

Varieties: Red Russian, an American heirloom also known as Ragged Jack, has red stems and blue-green leaves; *verdura,* a Dutch kale, is the most tender of all; *lacinato*, an Italian variety, resembles a fern and has a sweet flavor. Ornamental kale is generally much stronger in flavor and should be treated like mustard.

Buying: Kale grown for the supermarket usually has very thick stems (up to a half inch and even more) and is more like collards—to which all kale is closely related—than to garden-variety kale.

Nutritional Information: Kale is super high in the antioxidants A, C, and E and has good quantities of calcium, magnesium, iron, and many of the B vitamins. As with most dark brassicas, it is a nutritional powerhouse.

To Cook: When young, kale can be eaten raw; its flavor is a wonderful addition to mesclun. As it gets older, it takes more and more cooking, and although it can be quite tough unless cooked thoroughly, it has a rich, sweet, mild flavor and eventually becomes perfectly tender. Smaller (palm-sized) leaves can simply be cut up; those leaves larger than your hand should be separated from the stems (pages 7-8) and cooked separately.

Substitutes: Collards, which are extremely similar but flat-leaved and with a slightly more muted, subtle flavor; mustard, which has a similar texture but much sharper flavor; and any of the lesser-known brassicas such as tyfon.

Kale is among the darkest greens, very flavorful and nutritionally potent. It must be cooked sufficiently; undercooking yields a tough, bitter dish, whereas properly cooked, kale is sweet and tender. (Young kale is a different story; it's spicy and tender, with a welcome bitterness. However, young kale is almost the exclusive property of gardeners.)

Kale tolerates a wide range of temperatures—it can survive frost and thrives in southern heat—which makes it a year-round staple in much of the country. Countless European peasants relied on kale for much-needed nutrition through hard winter months in centuries gone by. Now, greens-savvy Americans look for kale and similar greens throughout the winter, where it is one of the few supermarket vegetables that actually retains some of its flavor.

Kale makes an excellent soup green and is a good addition to stir-fries; cut it into small pieces first, however, as directed earlier. Finally, kale can be stir-fried on its own: wash the leaves and dry them quickly, roll them up, and cut through the roll. Then stir-fry them in a bit of oil with some garlic and soy sauce or red pepper; if you use more oil, the dish becomes a fast, nutritious topping for pasta.

Kelp (kombu)

See Sea vegetables, pages 34-36.

Lettuce

Lactuca sativa

Varieties: Hundreds, but who's counting? Some are different in color, keeping power, size, number of days to maturity, disease and pest resistance, and so on. Although varieties are important (especially for gardeners), for all practical purposes, there are four major types:

1. Cabbage or crisphead lettuce: This is the familiar iceberg, rarely grown by gardeners and always sold in supermarkets; good texture, very mild flavor.
2. Cos or romaine lettuce: long, narrow leaves with fleshy, crunchy ribs; more flavorful than iceberg.
3. Butterhead lettuce: such as Boston or bibb, which forms a soft but fairly well-defined head with lots of loose outer leaves; very tender, delicate texture.

4. Looseleaf, bunching, or cutting lettuce: No real head; just a bunch of leaves joined at the base. Some of these, such as green-leaf or red-leaf, are sold in supermarkets, but this is the variety most popular with gardeners, who favor oak-leaf, Black-Seeded Simpson, and dozens of other varieties from which small pieces can be cut daily, resulting in a long-lived plant.

Buying: Needless to say, if you have a choice, buy local. Romaine and iceberg have decent keeping power, but most lettuces are quite fragile. It's not a problem if outer leaves are damaged as long as those leaves protected by the shell are fresh looking. The stem should not be brown.

Nutritional Information: All lettuce has decent amounts of beta carotene (generally, the darker the leaf the better, from this perspective). Looseleaf and romaine have a fair amount of calcium, a bit of vitamin C, and decent B-vitamin content, but lettuces do not compare favorably in nutritional value to most of the other leafy greens.

To Cook: Almost no one does anymore, but romaine makes a decent soup and is not bad when braised.

Like other greens, lettuce must be washed and dried before using it in a salad (*see* pages 6-7 for the best way to do this).

Substitutes: One for the other, freely. And obviously, when you're making a salad, anything goes.

Here's what Paula Peck, author of *The Art of Good Cooking,* wrote about salad: "To make it all wrong, take some iceberg lettuce…. Pour over it a concoction which is an orangey color, toss briefly, and you will have what is known as a tossed green salad. Sometimes the dressing is not orange, but a creamy white. However, the color doesn't make it taste much better."

The late Ms. Peck, who was prescient in many ways, wrote those words more than thirty-five years ago, then went on to describe the real thing—a mixture of as many greens as you can lay your hands on, dressed lightly with little more than olive oil, vinegar, pepper, and salt.

Caesar salad notwithstanding, the days of the one-lettuce salad are over. You might occasionally have a bowl of your favorite lettuce, simply dressed—especially in winter, when you have no choice—but you might just as readily have one of arugula, endive, or radicchio. The definite trend, however—and it's a good one—is toward the real mixed green salad, which contains not only lettuce but also many other raw greens. Gardeners clearly have an advantage here, but most supermarkets now sell a variety of greens, and some sell a mesclun mix. Lettuce, by itself, is not as important as it once was.

Which doesn't make it useless: Good lettuce still has a place in a mixed salad. It just doesn't dominate the way it once did.

Mâche (corn salad, lamb's lettuce, lamb's tongue, fetticus, field salad)

Valerianella locusta, V. olitoria, V. eriocarpa, or *Lactuca agnina*

Varieties: As you can see from the list, many. But they're not easy to distinguish. and since mâche is not especially common in stores, you take what you can get.

Buying: This plant is delicate; it should be bought fresh and kept cool. Leaves must not be limp.

Nutritional Information: Very high in beta carotene, especially among salad greens; decent amounts of vitamin C, calcium, and iron.

To Cook: A salad green that can stand alone—the small, dark, soft, tongue-shaped leaves are very tender and mildly flavorful—or can be mixed with others. It also can be cooked quickly like spinach, but we rarely have mâche in large enough quantity to justify this.

Substitutes: None really, although you can use any mild lettuce in most recipes calling for mâche.

Mâche is known as one of the "gourmet" salad greens, which means it is rare and expensive; too bad, because it's also a real treat. Gardeners like it because it can be grown almost through the winter and is among the first greens to be harvested in spring.

Mesclun (saladisi, misticanza, mescladisse)

There is a word in the Niçoise dialect that means mixture; that word is *mesclumo*. In southern France, the word is also used to apply to a mixture of a dozen or more wild and cultivated salad greens and herbs served with a simple vinaigrette. From this comes a tradition of brilliantly flavored, wonderfully textured salads.

From *mesclumo* also comes the word *mesclun*, and for current purposes, mesclun is a mixture of any greens—and flowers—that can be eaten raw as a salad. Period. Attempts to define mesclun by the number or types of greens will inevitably fail; there is no right or wrong. A good mix includes greens of various textures and flavors—not too heavy on strongly flavored greens such as arugula, mustard, or sorrel—some number of herbs, if possible, in small quantities, and any edible flowers that you can lay your hands on.

There are few greens and herbs that cannot, at some stage of their development, be used to make mesclun. The gardener can include young mustards, collards, kale, chard, even powerful herbs such as tarragon and lovage, in judicious amounts. Older greens that are too tough to eat raw are, of course, not suitable. The shopper who is presented with a packaged or pre-made mesclun mixture has, of course, no choice about what is included.

Mizuna (Japanese greens, spider mustard)

Brassica juncea

Varieties: I've only seen one.

Buying: If you see mizuna for sale in stores, buy greens that are less than four inches long if you want to eat them raw in salads. Larger greens are fine when cooked like dandelions or young mustard.

Nutritional Information: *See* Mustard, pages 31-32.

To Cook: As Mustard, pages 31-32.

Substitutes: Mustard, broccoli raab.

A mustard green that is increasingly showing up in mesclun, mizuna is a boon to home gardeners because it is productive, mild flavored, and very hardy. It's also lovely, sending out shoots of deeply serrated (hence, the name "spider mustard"), dark green leaves all summer.

Mustard (Chinese mustard, white mustard, black mustard, Indian mustard, mustard cabbage, mustard spinach, gai choy, etc.)

Brassica juncea, B. alba, b. hirta, b. nigra, b. rapa, etc.

Varieties: There are many, most available only to gardeners and people with access to gardens. Mustard greens are sold in supermarkets; Chinese mustards, which resemble a cross between broccoli raab and bok choi, are sold in Asian markets. Mizuna and the Japanese red mustard show up in high-class mesclun mixtures in restaurants and gourmet stores and are good in the home garden, as is tyfon (Holland greens) and edible chrysanthemum (*shingiku*). Two other varieties worth mentioning for gardeners: Green in Snow, a Chinese mustard that can tolerate frost (I grew it right through one unusually mild northeastern winter), and "Hon Tsai Tai" a Chinese version of broccoli raab.

Buying: Look for greens that are crisp and bright green without yellowing. Flower heads, if any, should be tight and green.

Nutritional Information: A big gun; not quite as potent as kale but supplied with good quantities of many antioxidants (especially beta carotene and vitamins C and E); several B vitamins; and calcium, iron, magnesium, potassium, and phosphorus.

To Cook: Young, mustard is great raw in salads; as it ages, it becomes almost intolerably hot, with a head-clearing quality like wasabe. Older leaves are a fine potherb, very similar to broccoli raab; good in stir-fries, too.

Substitutes: Cress for young leaves, broccoli raab for older. Most mustards can be used interchangeably.

These strong-flavored leafy greens are members of the huge *Cruciferae* family, which makes them close relatives of cabbage, broccoli, radishes, turnips, and so on. Many of the mustards can be found growing wild, and with a good wild food guide and the right season (usually late spring), you can find it easily. Leaves without flowers are good, but I especially like the easily recognized unopened flower heads, which taste much like broccoli seasoned with mustard.

Some mustards, especially the black and white varieties, are cultivated for their seeds, which are made into the condiment.

Nori (laver)

See Sea vegetables, pages 34-36.

Orach (mountain spinach)

Atriplex hortensis

Varieties: Red, white, or yellow are all available to the gardener. Leaves are attractive.

Buying: I've never seen orach in stores.

Nutritional Information: Unknown, but probably like that for spinach.

To Cook: As spinach.

Substitutes: Spinach.

A nice green to grow in the summer's heat, which it can take better than spinach can, orach is one of those ancient European greens you're still likely to be served from time to time in France, sometimes with other greens and sometimes under the nondescript name of *joutes*. In any case, it's a fine eating green and, if you grow the red variety, an especially good-looking one.

Pea shoots (pea greens)

Pisum sativum

Varieties: As many as there are of peas, which means dozens.

Buying: In Chinatown, where they are inexpensive, and specialty food stores, where they are not; should be bright green and undamaged.

Nutritional Information: Unknown.

To Cook: Small, thin leaves and stems can be tossed into salads; older leaves can be sautéed or stir-fried or added to soups or stews.

Substitutes: The flavor of pea shoots is unique.

These are no more than the greens of the common garden pea, "discovered" by chefs and soon thereafter by home cooks in 1992. I imagine that adventuresome gardeners knew these were edible and delicious at least five centuries earlier but can find no verification of this. The flavor is really excellent.

Purslane and winter purslane

(miner's lettuce, spring beauty)

Portulaca oleracea or *Claytonia perfoliata* or *Montia perfoliata*

Varieties: Cultivated varieties, which may be green or golden, larger leaves and more upright stems than plants from the wild, which are fleshy and prostrate.

Buying: Good luck! At some point purslane will enter the supermarket via the mesclun mix, but I have yet to see it in all but the most expensive markets. Look for very fleshy leaves and nice red stems.

Nutritional Information: Purslane is enormously rich in omega-3 fatty acids—it rivals fish oil in this quality—and is a good source of most antioxidants as well as iron, calcium, and phosphorus.

To Cook: Because purslane grows low to the ground and may be gritty, wash it well. The juicy leaves and stems as well as the flower buds can be eaten raw and are a great addition to the salad bowl. Purslane has a gelatinous quality when cooked, which makes it a fine green for soups and stews; cooked by itself, however, it has a bit of the same slippery quality as okra (which I like and you may, too—but many people do not).

Substitutes: None.

Purslane, which resembles a low-growing jade plant more than it does any familiar green, originated in the East and has been enjoyed in India and Persia for thousands of years. It grows wild in much of the United States and, like dandelion, is considered a noxious weed by many gardeners and homeowners. (I searched for it for years using Euell Gibbons's *Stalking the Wild Asparagus* and finally found it—in my garden, where I'd been pulling it up and tossing it on the compost.) In recent years it has been "discovered" as a delicious and highly nutritious vegetable.

Purslane has a refreshing lemony taste (the French say that it tastes like hazelnuts, which can only be good) and a wonderfully crunchy texture; because it is a bit bland, it combines well with some of the spicier greens.

Radicchio

See Chicory, pages 20-21.

Sea Vegetables (seaweed)

Varieties: Primarily Green algae such as nori (*Chlorophyta*); Brown algae, such as arame, hiziki, and kelp (*Phaeophyta*); and Red algae, such as dulse (*Rhodophyta*).

Buying: Unless you gather your own, sea vegetables are sold dried, in plastic or cellophane packages, in natural foods stores, some supermarkets and specialty stores, and by mail. For more detail, see below.

Nutritional Information: Most are very high in protein—nearly 34 percent for nori, around 20 percent for most others—which means they compare favorably to almost any other "high-protein" food. Sea vegetables are also high in vitamins A, B, C, and E and are among the few nonmeat sources of B-12. The biggest advantage of sea vegetables, however, is in their super mineral content: Most provide significant amounts of potassium, magnesium, phosphorous, iron, iodine (difficult to obtain from natural sources), other important minerals, and trace elements (rapidly disappearing from land vegetables because of soil depletion).

To Cook: See below.

Substitutes: Hiziki and arame are essentially interchangeable, as are alaria and wakame; otherwise, none.

Sea vegetables—the respectful term used to refer to those nutrition-packed plants commonly called "seaweed"—were undoubtedly among the first foods humans ate. Everywhere there is a fertile ocean there is evidence of a history of people foraging for sea vegetables. Sea vegetables remain a traditional food for both humans and animals in northern Europe, Russia, throughout the Arctic, and even in the high Andes, but until quite recently, the use of sea vegetables in this country was limited to a few ethnic groups and adherents of macrobiotic diets.

Now, however, sea vegetables are more widely available than ever and are making inroads at swank restaurants everywhere. They may not be as varied as "land" vegetables, but neither are they all dark and stringy or green and leafy. They vary by color, shape, texture, and flavor and can be used in salads, as a condiment, or on their own. To take them one at a time:

Nori (laver): The omnipresent sushi wrapper, nori can also be dry-roasted (in the oven or run, quickly and carefully, over an open flame), crumbled, and used as a condiment for soups, popcorn, or rice dishes. It can also be added to any stir-fry.

Kelp (kombu): This is the largest sea vegetable, growing up to 1,500 feet long (compare this to the tallest land plant, the Douglas fir, which is a mere 400 feet). Kelp is a key ingredient in dashi, the vegetarian stock that is one of the principal ingredients of Japanese cooking. Not often eaten on its own, kelp enhances the flavor and nutritional content of beans, soups, grains, and almost any other slow-simmered food.

Arame and hiziki: Dark, almost black, thin, and wiry, these are both mild tasting (hiziki is somewhat stronger). Soak in water before using—they will double in size—then use as a salad or add to salads, soups, or stews, sauté or braise it with other ingredients.

Alaria and wakame: These close relatives are pale green, almost transparent, and are best used in soups (cook for at least 20 minutes for best taste and texture), cooked with grains, and, after a brief soaking, in salads.

Dulse: Dulse is a lovely, brick red color with a mild sweet flavor. Even dried, it remains soft and pliable and can be eaten out of hand as a snack (a practice that remains common in parts of Ireland); it can also be pan-toasted and served like chips (as it was in New England taverns through the 1920s) and is good in sandwiches and salads after a brief rinse (it softens so quickly that actual soaking is unnecessary). It can also be included in chowders or other soups, where it cooks in five minutes or less.

Sorrel

(sour grass, garden sorrel, common sorrel, oseille, dock, spinach dock, curly dock, etc.)

Rumex acetosa, R. scutatus

Varieties: There are several varieties of sorrel; all have a sour taste due to the presence of oxalic acid. Common or garden sorrel has a sharp, sour flavor, whereas French sorrel (*R. scutatus*) is a bit milder with a lemony flavor. Wild sorrel, which looks like clover with tiny yellow flowers, is a refreshing nibble when you're hiking. Unlike most greens, sorrel is a very hardy perennial, making it great for gardeners.

Buying: You can sometimes buy bunches of fresh sorrel leaves and stems at farmers' markets and supermarkets, especially in the spring. The leaves, which are tender and smooth, are light green. Garden sorrel has narrow sword-shaped leaves, and the milder French sorrel has leaves that are wider at the base and shaped like shields.

Nutritional Information: Very high in vitamin C; European peasants have known for centuries that sorrel prevents scurvy.

To Cook: Sorrel is extremely delicate, even more so than spinach; use it as quickly as possible. Wash well to remove any grit. Raw, add only a few young leaves and stems to a salad; it is too sour to eat by itself. Sorrel will virtually disintegrate if overcooked, which makes it fine for soups and sauces; but if you want to eat it like spinach, you must plunge it into salted boiling water and remove it almost immediately.

Substitutes: Spinach, in some instances.

Sorrel, as Jane Grigson points out, is between a flavoring and a vegetable; it doesn't have much texture when cooked, but it has great flavor, and you can use it in large quantities. It is not only the basis of *schav* (which can be spelled about eight different ways)—the Eastern European sourgrass soup—but also of most instant soups that take advantage of its unusual flavor and thickening quality. Sorrel is also wonderful in salads and sandwiches; its sour quality cannot be provided by any other green (sorrel is related to rhubarb, as its taste may remind you). And it makes good sauces.

Sorrel also quenches thirst; you can make a lemonade-like drink: Cook the leaves until they fall apart, strain, add sugar to taste, and chill.

Spinach

Spinacia oleracea

Varieties: New Zealand spinach (*Tetragonia expansa*) is widely grown, commercially and by gardeners as a spinach substitute. It's a good one for two reasons: Its taste, texture, and nutritional composition are similar to spinach and it tolerates hot weather, which proper spinach does not. You've had New Zealand spinach; its leaves are flatter and more arrow shaped than those of the common plant. Of the many varieties of regular spinach available to the gardener, Bloomsdale Long Standing has the best heat resistance.

Buying: Many people think of spinach as a year-round vegetable, and indeed it is grown through the winter in California and elsewhere, packed in 10-ounce bags, and always in good supply. But the large, relatively tough, super-crinkly leaves of cellophane spinach cannot compare with the tender, flat-leaf variety grown by local farmers and gardeners. (When it is young, with stems an eighth of an inch in diameter or less, it wilts in a flash and requires almost no trimming.) Fresh spinach is delicate and should have a bright resiliency and fresh smell. It's easy enough to spot slimy, rotten leaves, and just as easy to avoid them.

Nutritional Information: Spinach is higher in protein than most vegetables, but it is known, rightly so, for its iron, calcium, B vitamins, and antioxidants such as beta carotene, and vitamins C and E.

To Cook: Clean spinach by pinching off any really tough stems from packaged spinach or by removing the crowns from bulk spinach. Then fill the sink or a large pot with water, dump in the spinach and swish it around, lift the green out to a bowl or colander, and change the water; repeat this process until the water is free of sand. The best way to cook spinach remains the source of some debate. Steaming with the water that clings to its leaves is inarguably fast and efficient, but the favored French, Italian, and Japanese method involves blanching spinach in a large pot of boiling water. The disadvantage here is that you have to bring a pot of water to the boil. However, this method offers good flavor and brilliant color, is foolproof, and takes no time at all once the water is boiling: Put the spinach into the pot, submerge it with a spatula or wooden spoon, and take it out with a skimmer or slotted spoon. Plunge it into cold water if you're not serving it immediately.

Substitutes: Chard can often fill in for spinach.

"In my youth," wrote the English author Jane Grigson, spinach "was shoveled into children as if their survival depended on it." This was a common experience on this side of the Atlantic as well, yet despite this, many of us have grown up to adore this lovely, oddly flavored green. Neither the ultimate bodybuilder (Popeye needed carbs, too) nor most-despised vegetable (Brussels sprouts gets worse press), spinach is among the first cooking greens of spring, wonderful when cooked as described above and then sautéed quickly in olive oil (and garlic, if you like), then sprinkled or drenched with fresh lemon juice; seasoned with soy, or ginger, or sesame, or a combination, and served cold; simmered lightly in a bit of browned butter; combined with tomatoes and made into pasta sauce; and so on.

Nutritionally, spinach is a curiosity: Although it is packed with calcium and iron, it also contains high levels of oxalates, substances that bind these and other minerals and prevent their absorption by the digestive system. Although oxalates make it unwise to count on spinach for calcium, zinc, magnesium, or other minerals, the green is still a valuable source of other nutrients such as vitamin A, the carotenes, and some of the more obscure phytochemicals that are currently coming to the fore in nutrition studies. So there is no reason to avoid spinach.

Swiss chard (chard, sea kale beet, leaf beet, ruby chard, red chard, white chard)

Beta vulgaris cicla

Varieties: Shoppers choose between white and red; gardeners rely on the old standbys Fordhook Giant (white) and Ruby Red. Beet greens are essentially a form of chard.

Buying: Chard stems are delicate; look for those that are unbruised. There is thick- and thin-stemmed chard. If you prefer the leaves, look for the latter (red chard is almost always thin-stemmed); if it's the stalks you're after, the former.

Nutritional Information: Chard is reasonably high in beta carotene, vitamin E, and some of the B vitamins, as well as iron, potassium, and magnesium.

To Cook: The leaves of chard are like spinach; the stems like bok choy. Start by washing it well, then cook leaf and stem either separately or together, allowing for the longer time needed for the stem to soften. Young chard leaves can be used raw in salads.

Substitutes: Beet greens, spinach.

A beet green gone wild, chard is a member of the beet family grown for its top rather than its bottom; it has been cultivated this way for at least 4,000 years. Chard has a thick midrib that is white, pink, or brilliant red; the leaves are sometimes ruffled and are deep green or green with rich scarlet veins. Unlike spinach, chard is heat-tolerant, which makes it a favorite among gardeners.

Chard is a fine green on its own, but like spinach, it has played a more important role in culinary tradition. It is often cooked in omelets, *frittate,* and pies, and frequently with meats, because its distinctive flavor and tender, pleasing texture complement those of other foods.

Turnip greens

Brassica rapa

Varieties: Most are the tops of white- or purple-topped turnips.

Buying: As with any leafy green, avoid turnip greens that have holes or bruises or that have yellowed.

Nutritional Information: The champion among greens when it comes to calcium, turnips are also a good source of beta carotene, vitamins C and E, many B vitamins, and some iron.

To Cook: Wash well; these can be sandy. Very young, they can be tossed into the salad bowl. Older, they can be steamed, boiled or—if they are not too tough—directly sautéed or stir-fried. Spring turnip greens, sweated in olive oil and dressed with lemon juice, are a Roman tradition.

Substitutes: Mustard.

I have tried cooking young turnips with their greens, and it was pleasant enough, but like beets, this is a case where the root and the top have different uses. Turnip greens, like mustard, collards, kale, and the like, are great on their own and rarely used in other dishes, but they are wonderful stir-fried with meats and in some soups.

Wakame

See Sea vegetables, pages 34-36.

Watercress (garden cress, peppergrass, upland cress)

Nasturtium officinalis, Lepidium sativum, Barbarea verna

Varieties: Gardeners have access to a wide variety of cresses; watercress is the only one sold in shops. It's also the most common variety found growing in the wild, always by running water, and often right through the winter.

Buying: Look for more leaves than stems; smaller plants are less peppery. Avoid yellowed leaves.

Nutritional Information: Good sources of beta carotene, vitamins C and B_1, and calcium.

To Cook: Wash well. Use in mixed salads, in a salad by itself, on sandwiches (watercress sandwiches are a classic tea accompaniment), as a garnish in cucumber or potato salad, or in soup. Cresses can also be steamed and served as a cooked green.

Substitutes: Arugala or nasturtium leaves.

Members of the mustard family, all cresses' small leaves with a sharp, peppery flavor go well with rich foods. Although cresses don't taste like arugula, their aggressive character is not dissimilar.

Wild Greens

Nearly twenty-five years ago, my lifelong partner and I simultaneously discovered Vermont and Euell Gibbons's classic, *Stalking the Wild Asparagus*. It was a brilliant marriage—we roamed meadows and woods, happily seeking, cooking, and eating dandelion crowns, milkweed, dock, chicory, nettles, mustard flowers, purslane, unopened day lilies, and whatever else we could lay our hands on. Our friends, for whatever reason, were not impressed, but we didn't care. Every new discovery was a triumph.

Roughly ten years later, we discovered children and gardening, and spent less time out foraging; it's more fun, we now think, to have control over the greens we eat, and there's no question that the radicchio from our garden tastes better than the chicory we once gathered from the fields.

Still, from time to time it's fun to go out and see what you can find. And although stumbling across a field of nice dandelions or a nettle patch is not quite as exciting as finding a hillside of wild strawberries, it's a fine way to obtain greens for dinner—definitely much better than a trip to the supermarket.

Although I've never become even mildly ill from eating the greens I've gathered from the wild (arguably, they're safer than the store-bought kind, since they are quite likely to be truly organic), misidentification could be a problem. Because identifying plants is beyond the ken of this book, I'll refer you to Gibbons's, which is far from comprehensive but still a pleasure, and to *A Field Guide to Edible Wild Plants,* by Lee Peterson (Houghton Mifflin), one of the Peterson Field Guides, which will likely tell you more than you want to know.

As for cooking wild greens when you get them home, follow a couple of basic rules: If they are tender, and the guidebooks don't tell you that they must be cooked to remove excess bitterness or a slightly poisonous substance, try them in a mesclun mix. If they are to be cooked—and some require boiling in one or more changes of water—finish them simply, perhaps by sautéing in a little butter. Milkweed greens, for example, which must be cooked, retain a unique flavor that most people like.

Many common wild greens, such as dandelion, orach, chicory, and purslane, are covered elsewhere in this book.

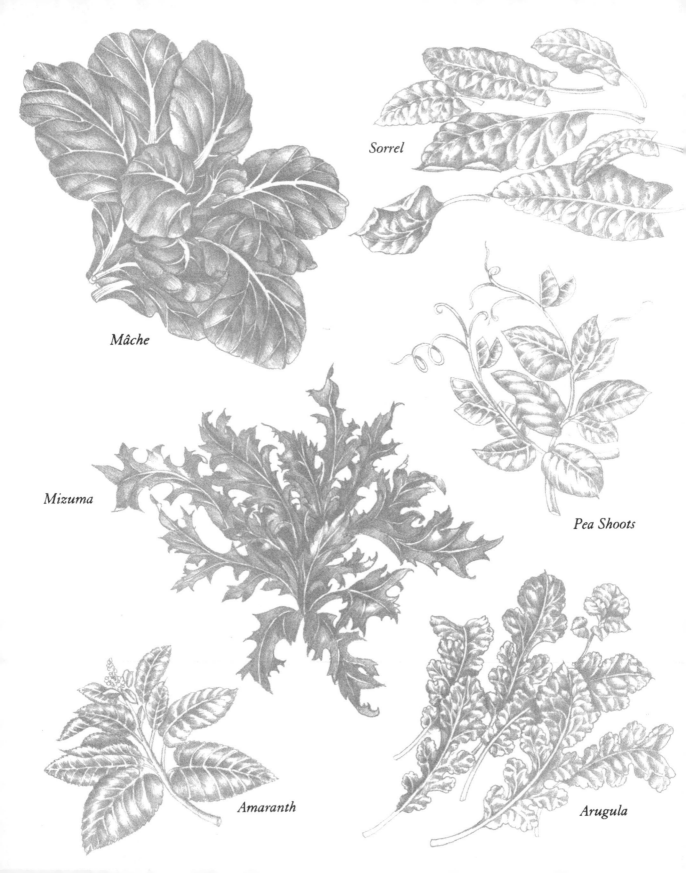

Mâche

Sorrel

Pea Shoots

Mizuma

Amaranth

Arugula

Watercress

Bibb Lettuce

Swiss Chard

Chicory

Mesclun

Kelp

Wakame

Hiziki

The Recipes

Soups

Clam Soup with Broccoli Raab and Linguica

½ pound dry garlicky
  sausage, such as linguica,
  kielbasa, or chorizo
4 cups light chicken or
  fish stock
1 pound broccoli raab,
  washed and trimmed
  according to the directions
  on pages 6-8

1 big starchy potato, peeled
  and thinly sliced
Salt and freshly ground
  black pepper
1 onion, minced
1 dozen littlenecks or
  other hard-shell clams,
  washed well

Makes 4 servings

Time: 30 minutes

Cut the sausage into bite-sized pieces and cook in a dry skillet until nicely browned, stirring occasionally.

Trim the broccoli raab of its tough ends, and peel the stalks if they are more than pencil-thick. Chop the broccoli raab coarsely, then combine it with the potato, sausage, and stock in a 3- or 4-quart saucepan. Simmer until the greens are tender. Season to taste, add the onions and clams, cover, and simmer until the clams are open, about 10 minutes. Serve immediately.

Other greens to use:

Collards or kale.

Garlic Soup with Spinach

4 tablespoons fruity olive oil
4 cloves garlic, peeled
4 thick slices French bread
5 to 6 plum tomatoes, skinned, seeded and chopped if fresh, chopped if canned

8 cups chicken broth, the best you can buy
8 to 10 ounces spinach, washed and trimmed according to the directions on pages 6-8

Makes 4 large servings
Time: About 30 minutes

Heat the olive oil over medium-low heat in a thick-bottomed pot that is large enough to hold the stock. Add the garlic cloves and cook, stirring and turning, until the garlic is toasted lightly brown. Remove the garlic to a plate and cook the bread on both sides until browned. Remove it.

Add the tomatoes and cook, stirring, for a minute or two, until they begin to break up. Add the stock, bring to a boil, lower the heat, and simmer for about 5 minutes. Remove the thickest stems from the spinach and discard; coarsely chop the spinach.

Add the spinach to the pot, and while it is cooking, spread each of the slices of bread with a clove of garlic. Pour the soup into a tureen and float the bread on top. Serve immediately.

Other greens to use:

Any of the tender greens, but nothing more bitter than spinach—try chard or beet greens, or tender Chinese cabbage like tah tsai.

⊚ ⊚ ⊚ ⊚ ⊚ ⊚ ⊚
I love all forms of garlic soup, but this one, which is extra rich, is my favorite. The sweetness of the sautéed garlic combines beautifully with the acidic spinach and tomatoes. A lovely lunch or light supper dish.
⊚ ⊚ ⊚ ⊚ ⊚ ⊚ ⊚

Creamy Kale Soup

1 large potato
1 clove garlic
4 cups light chicken stock or
  water
8 ounces kale leaves,
  stripped from the stalks
  (pages 7-8)

1 teaspoon fresh or ½ teaspoon dried marjoram or
  oregano
1 bay leaf
Salt and freshly ground
  pepper to taste

Makes 4 servings
Time: 30 minutes

Peel and roughly chop the potato; peel the garlic clove. Simmer both in 2 cups of the stock until soft, about 10 minutes; cool slightly. Rinse the kale, shake off the excess water, roll up a few leaves at a time, and chop them. Cook the kale in the remaining stock with the marjoram and bay leaf until tender, about 10 minutes. Remove the bay leaf. Purée the potato, garlic, and stock together; mixture will be thick. Stir it into the simmering kale, season with salt and pepper, and heat through. Serve immediately.

Other greens to use:

Broccoli raab, collards, mustard, turnip.

◦ ◦ ◦ ◦ ◦ ◦

Kale soup, a Portuguese specialty, is frequently spiced with sausage or thickened with cream. Here, however, its assertive flavor is complemented by marjoram, and puréed potato adds a pleasant texture without fat or meat.

◦ ◦ ◦ ◦ ◦ ◦ ◦

Soup of Turnip Greens and Scallops

8 cups light chicken stock

Salt

1 teaspoon ground black pepper, or more

1 pound turnip greens, washed and trimmed according to the directions on pages 6-8

1 large onion, peeled and chopped

1 tablespoon minced garlic

8 to 12 large sea scallops, cut in half horizontally to make 16 to 24 pieces

1/2 cup minced cilantro leaves

2 jalapeño chiles, seeded, stemmed, and minced

2 limes, quartered

Makes 4 servings

Time: 30 minutes

Bring the stock to a boil and add the salt and pepper. Chop the turnip greens roughly. Add them to the stock, along with the onion and garlic, and cook until tender, about 3 to 10 minutes depending on their toughness. Add the scallops and immediately ladle into bowls. Garnish with cilantro; pass the chile and limes at the table.

⊙ ⊙ ⊙ ⊙ ⊙ ⊙ ⊙

The heat of the soup is enough to cook these thinly sliced scallops right in the bowl.

⊙ ⊙ ⊙ ⊙ ⊙ ⊙ ⊙

Other greens to use:

Mustard, collards, kale, or broccoli raab.

Cabbage Soup, Asian Style

1 small head cabbage, about
  one pound
¼ cup peanut or vegetable oil
1 teaspoon minced ginger
4 cups light chicken or
  vegetable stock

2 tablespoons natural
  soy sauce
Salt and freshly ground black
  pepper to taste

Makes 4 servings
Time: About 30 minutes

Core the cabbage and shred it; heat the oil over high heat in a large skillet or wok until it begins to smoke. Toss the cabbage into the oil and cook, stirring frequently, until the cabbage begins to brown. Add the ginger and cook, stirring, another minute or two.

Add the stock, bring to a simmer, lower the heat, and cook, stirring every now and then, until the cabbage is tender but not mushy, 10 to 20 minutes. Add the soy sauce, season to taste, and serve.

A fast, meatless cabbage soup with few ingredients and lots of flavor.

Variation

Cabbage Soup, northern European Style: Sauté the cabbage in ¼ cup butter (½ stick) rather than oil, until nicely browned. Add 2 tablespoons brown sugar, ¼ teaspoon allspice, and broth. Season to taste and serve.

Other greens to use:

Any cabbage, including the Chinese cabbages. You could also make this with kale, collards, or broccoli raab.

Kale Soup with Soy and Lime

2 tablespoons peanut oil
1 cup minced onion
1 pound kale, washed and
  trimmed according to the
  directions on pages 6-8
2 tablespoons minced garlic
6 cups light chicken or
  vegetable stock

1 tablespoon soy sauce
Salt to taste
1 fresh jalapeño, optional,
  deveined, seeded, and
  minced
1 lime, cut into eighths

Makes 4 servings
Time: About 20 minutes

Heat the oil in a large pot over medium heat. Add the onion and cook, stirring occasionally, until it begins to brown. While it is cooking, remove and discard any thick stems from the kale and chop the rest.

When the onion is tender and golden, add the garlic. Cook a minute or two and add the stock. Bring to a boil, lower the heat, add the soy sauce, and taste for salt; add some if necessary. Add the kale to the simmering broth and cook until it is tender, about 10 minutes. Correct the seasoning (you may prefer to add more soy sauce rather than more salt) and serve, passing the minced jalapeño and pieces of lime.

Other greens to use:

Bok choi, broccoli raab, collards, mustard, or turnips.

○ ○ ○ ○ ○ ○

Another Asian-spiced soup that is fast and really delicious. Use fish sauce (nuoc mam) instead of soy sauce if you have some.

○ ○ ○ ○ ○ ○

Coconut Curry Soup with Chard

2 cups dried, unsweetened
  coconut
2 cups boiling water
2 tablespoons peanut or
  vegetable oil
1 tablespoon minced garlic
1 medium onion, minced
1 teaspoon curry powder

1 pound red or green chard,
  washed and trimmed
  according to the directions
  on pages 6-8
Salt and freshly ground black
  pepper
1/4 cup minced fresh cilantro

Makes 4 servings
Time: About 30 minutes

Place the coconut in a blender and cover it with 1 cup boiling water. Cover the blender, and holding the top on with a folded towel to reduce the possibilities of scalding, blend for 20 seconds or so. Let the mixture sit for a few minutes, then strain, pressing to extract as much liquid as possible.

Heat the oil over medium heat in a 10- or 12-inch skillet that can later be covered. Add the garlic and onion and cook, stirring, until the onion softens. Add the curry powder and cook, stirring, another 30 seconds or so.

Add the coconut milk and two cups of water; stir, bring to a boil, and lower the heat to a simmer. Chop the chard roughly and add it to the soup; keep at a simmer and stir occasionally as the chard wilts. Add salt and pepper to taste and cook until the chard is tender, about 10 minutes. Serve hot, garnished with cilantro.

Other greens to use:

Bok choi.

○ ○ ○ ○ ○ ○ ○
This is more like a thick stew than like a soup; add some cayenne to the spice mixture if you like your food on the hot side.
○ ○ ○ ○ ○ ○ ○

Simple Cabbage Soup with Tomatoes and Vinegar

6 cups light chicken or
vegetable stock

12 scallions, trimmed and
roughly chopped

Salt and freshly ground black
pepper

1 pound white or Savoy
cabbage, cored and shredded

2 or 3 ripe tomatoes, peeled,
seeded, and roughly
chopped, or about 1½ cups
canned plum tomatoes

1 tablespoon rice or wine
vinegar

Makes 4 servings

Time: About 40 minutes

Heat the stock in a kettle; reserve some of the scallion greens and add the rest of the scallions to the stock, along with salt and pepper to taste, the cabbage, and the tomatoes. Simmer, stirring occasionally, until the cabbage is tender and the tomatoes have fallen apart, about 30 minutes.

Add the vinegar and check the seasoning; you may add more vinegar if you like. Mince the reserved scallion greens and use them to garnish the soup. Serve immediately.

Other greens to use:

You can make this with any cabbage, including the Chinese varieties, but I like it best with plain old head cabbage.

Corn and Kale Stew

4 ears of fresh corn
2 cups chicken or vegetable
  stock or water
Salt and freshly ground black
  pepper

1 pound kale, washed and
  trimmed according to the
  directions on pages 6-8
2 tablespoons unsalted butter,
  optional

Makes 4 servings
Time: About 40 minutes

Shuck the corn; using a fork or knife, scrape the kernels off the cobs. Do not worry about getting every last bit. Cut the cobs into chunks.

Simmer the cobs in the stock if you have it, in water if you do not, for about 10 minutes. Season the stock to taste. Chop the kale coarsely and add it to the stock; cover and simmer for about 10 to 15 more minutes, until the kale is tender but not mushy. Add the corn kernels and simmer another minute or two more, just to heat through. Add the butter if you like, stir it in, and serve.

⊙ ⊙ ⊙ ⊙ ⊙ ⊙
A great dish for those who can take advantage of late-summer gardens—very simple with clean, essential flavors.
⊙ ⊙ ⊙ ⊙ ⊙ ⊙ ⊙

Other greens to use:

Almost any fresh cooking green you can get your hands on, but nothing too-too bitter: Beet greens, chard, collards, or mustard would be my first choices after kale.

Miso Soup with Spinach and Tofu

1 5- to 6-inch piece of dried
kelp (kombu)
5 cups water
1/2 cup dried bonito flakes,
optional
8 to 10 ounces spinach,
washed and trimmed
according to the directions
on page 39

3 tablespoons miso (Japanese
bean curd paste, available at
Asian markets and health
food stores)
1/2 pound soft or silken tofu,
carefully cut into small
cubes
Several thin slivers of lemon
peel for garnish

Makes 4 servings
Time: About 40 minutes, much less with
premade stock

Wipe the kelp with a damp towel, put it in a pot with the water, and turn the heat to medium. Without ever letting the water boil, heat the kelp for about 20 minutes, or until it is tender. Remove the kelp and either discard it, reserve it for another use, or chop it up and return it to the stock later. If you are using bonito flakes toss them in and let the mixture sit for 5 minutes; strain and discard the bonito flakes.

Chop the spinach coarsely and add it to the broth; while it is cooking (still at a gentle simmer), remove a bit of the broth and mix it with the miso to thin the latter. Stir the miso back into the soup, add the tofu, and cook another minute or 2 before serving. Top with the lemon peel.

Variation

Miso Soup with Spinach and Shiitakes: Omit tofu; trim and slice 6 fresh shiitake mushrooms and sauté in 2 tablespoons peanut oil over medium-high heat until slightly crisp and wilted. Add them at the last minute, after stirring in the miso.

Other greens to use:

Chard (discard large stems), cress, dandelion, or mizuna.

⊚ ⊚ ⊚ ⊚ ⊚ ⊚ ⊚

You can make miso soup with chicken or beef broth, but it's so simple to make dashi—the Japanese stock that forms the basis of many soups—that you might as well be authentic. Dashi can be made with or without bonito flakes, a convenient, flavorful form of dried fish sold in almost all Asian markets.

⊚ ⊚ ⊚ ⊚ ⊚ ⊚ ⊚

Chicken Soup with Chinese Cabbage and Thin Noodles

Either:

    6 cups chicken stock

    1 pound boneless chicken breast

Or:

    6 cups water

    1 whole chicken breast, with bone

    1 carrot

    1 onion

And:

    Salt

    1 pound bok choi, washed and trimmed according to the directions on pages 6-8

    1 tablespoon peanut oil

    2 cloves garlic, minced

    1 teaspoon minced ginger

    1 tablespoon soy sauce

    8 ounces dried thin Chinese egg noodles

Makes 4 servings

Time: 30 to 60 minutes

If you have stock already, cut the chicken breast into slivers and simmer it in the stock for about 2 minutes; don't worry if it isn't quite done. Remove the chicken and keep the stock warm.

If you are starting from scratch, bring the water to a boil and add the chicken breast, carrot, and onion; lower the heat and simmer for about 30 minutes. Remove the chicken and the vegetables. Run the chicken under cold water until it is cool enough to handle, then pull it off the bone; discard the skin and the vegetables and return the chicken bones to the stock, allowing them to simmer while you prepare the other ingredients. Cut the chicken meat into slivers; don't worry if it isn't quite done.

Bring a large pot of water to a boil and salt it. Heat a wok or large skillet over medium-high heat. Cut the cabbage into 1- to 2-inch pieces, smaller for the stems, larger for the leaves. Add the peanut oil to the wok and stir-fry the garlic and ginger for 15 seconds, then add the cabbage. Raise the heat to high and stir-fry the cabbage until fairly tender, about 10 minutes. Add the soy sauce, taste for salt, and turn off the heat.

Cook the noodles in the boiling water until still al dente; drain. Remove any chicken bones from stock. Add the noodles, cabbage, and chicken to the stock and cook until heated through. Serve immediately, passing additional soy sauce at the table.

If you don't have chicken stock on hand, start with a piece of chicken that is on the bone; otherwise, this soup will be thin and watery.

Other greens to use:

Broccoli raab, Savoy cabbage, chard, or mustard.

Spinach and Lentil Soup

1 cup lentils
Water as needed
1 bay leaf
Several sprigs of fresh thyme,
    or a few pinches of dried
    thyme
2 tablespoons olive oil
1 onion, peeled and chopped
1 teaspoon minced garlic

1/4 teaspoon cayenne pepper,
    optional
1/2 teaspoon cumin
1 pound spinach, washed and
    trimmed according to the
    directions on page 39
Salt and freshly ground black
    pepper

Makes 4 to 6 servings
Time: About 45 minutes

Wash and pick over the lentils carefully. Place them in a pot with water to cover the bay leaf and the thyme; bring to a boil and simmer while you prepare the other ingredients.

Chop the spinach coarsely. Heat the olive oil over medium-low heat in a 12-inch skillet, preferably non-stick. Add the onion and cook, stirring, until it softens. Add the garlic, cayenne, and cumin, and stir. Add the spinach, raise the heat to medium high, and cook, stirring, until it wilts, about 5 minutes.

When the lentils are tender—they usually take about 30 minutes; fish out the bay leaf and the thyme sprigs and pour the spinach mixture into them. Season with salt and pepper and serve.

Variations

Chard and Lentil Soup: Substitute 1 teaspoon ground coriander for the cayenne and cumin, and finish the soup with 2 tablespoons freshly squeezed lemon juice.

Spinach and Chickpea Soup: Use 2 cups canned chickpeas, or soak 1 cup chickpeas overnight before cooking with bay leaf and thyme until tender. Proceed as in original recipe.

Other greens to use:

Nothing too tough, but otherwise the choices are many: arugula, cress, dandelion, mizuna, or young broccoli raab, collards, kale, mustard, or turnip.

Sorrel and Potato Soup

4 to 5 cups rich chicken stock
1 medium potato, peeled and
   quartered
1 onion, peeled and quartered
1 clove garlic
3 cups sorrel leaves, washed
   and trimmed according to
   the directions on pages 6-8

Salt and freshly ground black
   pepper
Minced parsley for garnish

Makes 4 servings

Time: About 45 minutes, plus time to chill

Heat the stock and add the potato, onion, and garlic. Cook
until the potato is quite soft, 20 to 30 minutes. Chop the sorrel and
add it to the soup; cook just until it wilts, a couple of minutes. Pass
the mixture through a food mill or purée in a blender (you can
wait until it's cooled off if you like; it's safer that way). Adjust seasoning and reheat or chill to serve cold (remember that cold foods
take more salt). Garnish with parsley before serving.

o o o o o o o

*You can serve this hot or cold,
like a Vichyssoise.*

o o o o o o o

Variation

Sorrel and Cucumber Soup: Substitute a peeled cucumber for
the potato and omit the onion; add ½ cup heavy cream before
puréeing. If you choose to serve this version hot, rewarm
carefully and do not allow to boil.

Other greens to use:

Nothing tastes like sorrel, but arugula, cress, dandelion, mizuna,
or spinach would all make similar if different-tasting soups.

Tortellini and Chard in Broth

6 cups full-flavored chicken
stock
2 carrots, peeled and sliced
into thin rings
1 onion, peeled and diced
Salt and freshly ground
black pepper
About 1 pound chard, red or
green, washed and trimmed
according to the directions
on pages 6-8

1 pound tortellini
2 tablespoons minced parsley
for garnish
Freshly grated Parmesan

Makes 4 servings

Time: About 30 minutes

Bring the stock to a boil, lower the heat, and add the carrots and the onion; simmer until the carrots are just about tender, 10 to 20 minutes depending on the thickness of the slices. Taste and season as needed. Meanwhile, bring a pot of water to boil for the tortellini.

Chop the chard coarsely and add it to the simmering broth. Cook the tortellini in the pot of boiling water until nearly tender, checking frequently. Drain it and add it to the soup. Check and correct seasoning if necessary, spoon into bowls, garnish with parsley, and pass the Parmesan at the table.

⊙ ⊙ ⊙ ⊙ ⊙ ⊙ ⊙
Because this dish has so few ingredients, it's worth your while to use the best possible chicken stock.
⊙ ⊙ ⊙ ⊙ ⊙ ⊙ ⊙

Other greens to use:

Something about chard makes this soup special; I wouldn't go any further than beet greens for a substitute.

Watercress Soup

4 cups watercress, washed
    and trimmed according to
    the directions on pages 6-8
2 tablespoons butter

4 cups good chicken stock
Salt and freshly ground black
    pepper
2 cups milk

Makes 4 servings
Time: About 30 minutes

Chop the cress coarsely. Heat the butter in a pot and sauté the cress until it wilts. Add the stock, bring almost to a boil, lower the heat, and cook briefly, until the cress is tender. Put through a food mill and return to the heat. Season to taste, add the milk, heat through, and serve immediately.

Variation

Watercress Soup with Potatoes: Before sautéing the cress, add 2 peeled and coarsely chopped potatoes and 1 peeled and coarsely chopped onion to the melted butter. Cover and cook over medium-low heat, stirring occasionally, until the onions and potatoes are nearly tender, about 15 minutes. Add the watercress and proceed according to the original recipe.

Other greens to use:

Arugula, sorrel, or spinach; the character will change with any of these, but the soup will still be quite good.

⊙ ⊙ ⊙ ⊙ ⊙ ⊙ ⊙

If you'd like to make watercress (or spinach, arugula, or sorrel) soup without milk, follow the directions for the Creamy Kale Soup on page 53. You need not purée either of these soups, but I love the creamy texture.

⊙ ⊙ ⊙ ⊙ ⊙ ⊙ ⊙

Soup of Greens, Beans, and Rice

½ pound white beans, soaked
    for about 8 hours and
    drained
Several sprigs of fresh thyme,
    or about 1 teaspoon dried
    thyme
1 bay leaf
1 whole onion

Salt and freshly ground black
    pepper
4 cups stock or water
3 cups collards, washed and
    trimmed according to the
    directions on pages 6-8
1 cup rice
1 teaspoon minced garlic

Makes 4 servings
Time: About 1½ hours, including
cooking the beans

Put the beans, thyme, bay leaf, and onion in a large pot and cover with water. Bring to a boil and simmer until tender, adding water as necessary. Strip the collard leaves from the stems. Chop the stems into 1-inch sections and chop the leaves coarsely; keep them separate.

When the beans are tender, about an hour later, remove the onion, bay leaf, and fresh thyme sprigs. Season to taste and add the stock or water; bring to a boil and add the collard stems. Cook, stirring, until the stems are barely tender, about 20 minutes. Add the greens and the rice and cook, stirring occasionally until the rice is tender, about 15 minutes. Add a bit more water if necessary (this is a soup) and stir in the garlic. Cook one minute, check the seasoning and correct it if necessary, and serve.

○ ○ ○ ○ ○ ○ ○

You can make this soup with stock or with water, as you like; it is, of course, more flavorful with stock. It's a hearty soup as it stands, but if you're interested in turning it into a big-time stew, see the variation that follows, which serves at least six.

○ ○ ○ ○ ○ ○ ○

Variation

Beans, Greens, and Rice Stew with Meat: Cook the beans with a ham bone, a hunk of bacon, a piece of beef short rib or flanken, or all three. Fish the meat out when the beans are done and cut it into pieces, discarding the bones and fat, if any. Add 2 or 3 potatoes, peeled and cut up, along with the collard stems, and if you like, sauté 2 or 3 sweet Italian sausages until nicely browned, cut them up, and add them to the stew along with the garlic.

Other greens to use:

Kale, mustard, or turnips.

Spinach and Egg Soup

1 pound spinach, washed and
   trimmed according to the
   directions on page 39
2 tablespoons butter
Salt and freshly ground black
   pepper

Dash of freshly grated
   nutmeg
5 to 6 cups good chicken stock
2 eggs
1 cup freshly grated
   Parmesan

Makes 4 servings

Time: About 30 minutes

Steam or parboil the spinach until it wilts (pages 8-9). Cool it under cold water, squeeze it dry, and chop.

Melt the butter in a 4- to 6-quart saucepan over medium heat. Add the spinach, salt, pepper, and nutmeg. Add the stock and bring to a gentle simmer. Beat the eggs with half the Parmesan and add them to the soup. Cook, stirring occasionally, until the eggs are cooked and soup is thick. Serve with bread, passing the remaining Parmesan at the table.

⊙ ⊙ ⊙ ⊙ ⊙ ⊙

A rich, eggy dish that could easily serve as a rather nice dinner for two, as long as you had plenty of bread.

⊙ ⊙ ⊙ ⊙ ⊙ ⊙ ⊙

Other greens to use:

Cress.

Salads

Partridge Salad with Walnuts and Port

1 wild partridge

1 tablespoon light
  vegetable oil

2 tablespoons butter or
  olive oil

1 clove garlic, minced

$^1/_2$ cup walnuts or pecans,
  coarsely crumbled (do not
  chop fine)

$^1/_2$ cup port or cassis

6 cups washed assorted tender
  greens; a mesclun mixture
  (page 30) is ideal

$^1/_2$ cup or more light
  vinaigrette, such as the one
  on page 95

Makes 4 servings

Time: Less than 30 minutes

Use a small, sharp knife to remove the meat from the bird (discard the bones or reserve them for stock); cut into half-inch dice. In a small skillet over medium-high heat, sauté the meat in the vegetable oil for a minute or two; do not overcook.

Wipe out the skillet. Add the butter, still over medium-high heat; when the foam subsides, add the garlic and cook for a minute. Add the walnuts and stir for 30 seconds. Add the port and let it bubble out until the mixture is syrupy, stirring occasionally. Turn off the heat and return the meat to the pan.

When ready to eat, dress the salad with the vinaigrette and toss; add more vinaigrette if necessary. Warm the partridge mixture briefly, scatter on top of the salad, and serve.

⊙ ⊙ ⊙ ⊙ ⊙ ⊙

In the fall, you can buy fresh, wild Scottish partridge by mail, and the birds are sometimes available frozen year-round (Call: 1-800-DARTAGNAN). The price is high, but the flavor is intense; one small bird has an enormous impact on a salad such as this one, which makes a sensational lunch or light dinner dish.

⊙ ⊙ ⊙ ⊙ ⊙ ⊙

Wakame and Cucumber Salad

1 medium cucumber, as fresh
   as possible
½ cup wakame
2 tablespoons rice vinegar

½ teaspoon sugar, optional
1 teaspoon high-quality
   soy sauce

Makes 4 servings
Time: 15 minutes

Bring a pot of water to a boil while you soak the wakame in cool water for 10 minutes. Plunge the wakame into the boiling water, remove immediately, then plunge it into cold water. Dry the wakame, trim any tough parts, and chop.

Cut the cucumber in half, lengthwise; if it has lots of seeds, scrape them out. Slice it as thin as possible. Mix the cucumber and wakame. Combine the remaining ingredients and pour over the vegetables. Chill until ready to serve.

Other greens to use:

Hijiki, arame.

⊙ ⊙ ⊙ ⊙ ⊙ ⊙
This is based on a traditional Japanese dish that remains popular today. Note that this high-flavor salad contains no added fat.
⊙ ⊙ ⊙ ⊙ ⊙ ⊙

Cress and Barley Salad with Dill Vinaigrette

½ cup pearled barley

1 medium cucumber,
   peeled if you prefer

6 tablespoons olive oil

2 tablespoons white wine
   vinegar

2 tablespoons minced
   fresh dill

Salt and pepper to taste

3 cups watercress, trimmed,
   washed, and dried according
   to the directions on pages 6-8

Makes 4 servings

Time: 30 minutes

Cook the barley in 3 or 4 cups of salted boiling water until tender; drain, rinse briefly in cool water, and set aside. Cut the cucumber in half, scoop out the seeds if there are a lot of them, then chop it into a fairly fine dice.

Whisk together the olive oil and vinegar, add the dill, and season with salt and pepper. Taste for seasoning and correct if necessary. Chop the cress coarsely and toss it with the barley. Top with the chopped cucumber, drizzle with the dressing, and serve.

Other greens to use:

Dandelion and mizuna are ideal. That same slightly tough and mild spiciness can also be found in very young kale or collards, usually available only to the gardener.

Salade Niçoise

4 to 6 cups assorted lettuces and other salad greens, trimmed, washed, and dried according to the directions on pages 6-8; or a typical mesclun mix (page 30)

2 cans tuna in water or olive oil, flaked

2 hard-cooked eggs, peeled and cut into slices

2 cups green beans, steamed for 4 minutes, rinsed, and chilled (you may omit these if pressed for time)

1 cup good black olives (oil-cured are good for this)

3 ripe tomatoes, cut into quarters or eighths

1 bell pepper (any color but green), cleaned and cut into rings

6 anchovies, optional

1 teaspoon capers, optional

For the vinaigrette:

$1/2$ cup extra virgin olive oil, approximately

$1/8$ cup good vinegar, or a little more

Salt and freshly ground black pepper to taste

1 small shallot, minced

1 teaspoon of Dijon mustard

Makes 4 to 6 servings

Time: About 45 minutes, far less if you prepare some ingredients in advance

Arrange all the salad ingredients nicely on a platter—greens on the bottom, topped with tuna, pepper, green beans, tomatoes, egg slices, and olives, with the anchovies and capers sprinkled over all. Or—less attractive but definitely easier to serve—toss all the ingredients together.

Make the vinaigrette by adding the vinegar to the oil, along with the salt and pepper, shallot, and mustard. Stir and taste. Add more vinegar if necessary and adjust seasoning. Stir or shake vigorously, pour over the salad, and serve.

Other greens to use:

Anything that can be eaten raw.

⊚ ⊚ ⊚ ⊚ ⊚ ⊚

There are certain basics that are essential in Salade Niçoise— canned tuna fish, tomatoes, anchovies, and, of course, greens. Hard boiled eggs are traditional—as are capers, olives, and onions—but their omission causes no great hardship. Feel free to improvise, but always use the best olive oil you have for the vinaigrette.

⊚ ⊚ ⊚ ⊚ ⊚ ⊚

Thai Beef Salad with Boston Lettuce

8 to 10 ounces beef tenderloin
  or sirloin

1 large or 2 small heads
  Boston lettuce, trimmed,
  washed, and dried according to the directions on
  pages 6-8

2 tablespoons minced
  fresh cilantro

1 small red onion, peeled and
  sliced into thin rings

1 small cucumber (preferably
  unwaxed and unpeeled),
  thinly sliced

4 tablespoons freshly
  squeezed lime juice

1 tablespoon Thai or
  Vietnamese fish sauce
  (available in Asian markets)
  or soy sauce

$1/4$ teaspoon cayenne, or
  to taste

$1/2$ teaspoon sugar

Makes 3 to 4 servings

Time: 30 minutes, tops

Broil or grill the meat until medium rare, about 10 to 12 minutes; set aside to cool.

Tear the lettuce, then mix it with the cilantro, onion, and cucumber. Mix together the lime juice, fish sauce, cayenne, and sugar; toss the lettuce with this dressing, reserving about a table-spoon.

Slice the beef thinly, capturing as much of its juice as you can; lay the slices over the salad. Mix the beef juice with the re-served dressing, drizzle over the beef, and serve.

Other greens to use:

Almost any lettuce, although I do think that the delicacy of Boston is unsurpassed here.

☉ ☉ ☉ ☉ ☉ ☉

You will not find a way to get more satisfaction out of a small piece of beef than this, nor are you likely to find a lighter, fresher beef dish. You can substitute fresh parsley or mint (or a combination) for the cilantro, but do not try this dish with dried herbs. Serve with plain white rice.

☉ ☉ ☉ ☉ ☉ ☉

Salad in Pita Bread with Tahini Dressing

2 carrots, peeled and grated

1 cup alfalfa sprouts

1 quarter head of red cabbage, shredded

¼ cup roughly chopped pecans or walnuts

1 cup sesame tahini

¼ cup lemon juice

1 clove garlic

¼ cup water, more or less

Salt and freshly ground pepper to taste

6 leaves of romaine lettuce, trimmed, washed, and dried according to the directions on pages 6-8

2 ripe tomatoes, cut into eighths, only if they are in season

6 pita breads, cut in half

Mix together the carrots, sprouts, cabbage, and walnuts. Put the tahini in a blender or food processor with the garlic and lemon juice and process until smooth; add water gradually, processing until creamy, then add salt and pepper to taste.

Toss the vegetable with the lettuce, tomato, and dressing, then pile into pitas and serve immediately.

A light, flavorful vegetarian sandwich, great for a fast lunch.

Other greens to use:

The combination of crisp greens with distinct flavors—cabbage and romaine—is pleasant here, but you can use any lettuces or other raw greens you like.

Fried Chile-spiced Clam Salad

6 tablespoons extra virgin
   olive oil

2 tablespoons balsamic
   vinegar

2 teaspoons Dijon-style
   mustard

3 tablespoons peanut, olive, or
   vegetable oil

20 to 25 fresh littleneck or
   other hard-shell clams,
   shucked

$^1/_2$ cup corn meal

2 tablespoons chile powder

Salt and pepper

6 cups mixed greens, your
   choice, trimmed, washed,
   and dried according to the
   directions on pages 6-8

Makes 4 servings

Time: 30 minutes

Mix together the olive oil, balsamic vinegar, and mustard.

Heat a 12-inch non-stick skillet over medium-high heat for about 5 minutes. Add the peanut oil. Season the flour with chile powder, salt, and pepper. When the oil is hot—a pinch of flour will sizzle—dredge the clams and add them, a couple at a time, to the skillet. Raise heat to high and cook until golden, turning once, about 2 minutes total.

Drain the clams on paper towels and toss the greens with the dressing. Divide the greens among 4 plates and top each with a portion of clams. Serve immediately.

⊙ ⊙ ⊙ ⊙ ⊙ ⊙

This combination contains the elements that almost everyone loves: It's spicy, it's crunchy, it's cool, and it's moist. A winner, which can also be made with oysters or chunks of any white-fleshed fish or chicken.

⊙ ⊙ ⊙ ⊙ ⊙ ⊙ ⊙

Grilled Chicken Salad with Mesclun

1 pound boneless chicken
  breast, about 4 pieces
1/4 cup soy sauce
6 to 8 cups assorted salad
  greens

Juice of 1 large lemon
1/2 cup fruity extra virgin
  olive oil, approximately
1 teaspoon dark sesame oil

Makes 4 servings
Time: About 60 minutes,
including marinating time

Pound the chicken lightly between two pieces of waxed paper so that it is of uniform thickness. Soak the pieces in the soy sauce while you ready a charcoal or preheat a gas grill and wash the greens according to the directions on pages 6-7.

Grill the chicken very quickly, on the hottest part of the grill; it should take no more than 2 minutes per side to become lightly browned. Dress the greens with the lemon juice and olive oil, then cut up the chicken and scatter it atop the salad. Sprinkle with the sesame oil and serve.

⊙ ⊙ ⊙ ⊙ ⊙ ⊙ ⊙

This is a great summer salad, when greens are abundant, and you've got the grill going full time.

⊙ ⊙ ⊙ ⊙ ⊙ ⊙ ⊙

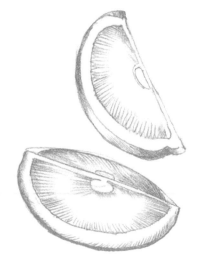

Shrimp Salad with Arugula "Pesto"

8 cups water

Salt and freshly ground black pepper

1 onion, cut in half but unpeeled

3 cloves garlic, lightly crushed

1 carrot, peeled and cut into chunks

½ bunch parsley

2 bay leaves

1 tablespoon vinegar

½ cup dry white wine

2 pounds medium-to-large shrimp, shell on

2 cups arugula, trimmed, washed, and dried according to the directions on pages 6-8

1 clove garlic

2 tablespoons walnuts or pine nuts

½ cup extra virgin olive oil, more or less

¼ cup minced parsley

Lemon wedges

Serves 3 or 4

Time: 30 minutes

Simmer together the water, salt, pepper, onion, garlic, carrot, parsley, bay leaves, vinegar, and white wine for about 10 minutes. Add the shrimp and simmer until they begin to turn pink, about 2 or 3 minutes. Turn off the heat and let the shrimp cool in the water for 10 minutes.

Remove any tough stems from the arugula. Place it in a food processor or blender with some salt, the garlic, nuts, and ¼ teaspoon pepper. Add ¼ cup olive oil and pulse. With the motor running, add additional olive oil to make a creamy sauce.

Remove the shrimp from the stock (strain and reserve it for another use), shell them, and toss with the minced parsley, a few tablespoons of olive oil, and salt and pepper to taste. Top with the arugula pesto and serve with lemon wedges.

◎ ◎ ◎ ◎ ◎ ◎
With its clean, bright flavor, this dish is worlds away from American shrimp salad.
◎ ◎ ◎ ◎ ◎ ◎

Other greens to use:

The flavor of watercress is nearly as powerful and distinctive as that of arugula. Anything else would get lost in the shuffle (of course you could use basil for the pesto).

Doc's Salad of Arugula, Grapefruit, and Mandarin Oranges

1 grapefruit
½ cup fruity extra virgin olive oil
¼ cup freshly squeezed lemon juice
¼ cup chopped parsley
½ teaspoon minced garlic
Salt and freshly ground black pepper to taste

1 small can mandarin oranges, drained
1 small red onion, halved and very thinly sliced
2 bunches arugula (about half a pound), trimmed, washed, and dried according to the directions on pages 6-8
6 to 8 whole basil leaves

Makes 4 servings
Time: 15 minutes

Remove the outer peel from the grapefruit, separate into sections, remove the transparent peel from sections if you like, and cut the sections into small pieces.

In a small bowl, whisk together the olive oil, lemon juice, parsley, garlic, salt, and pepper.

Combine the fruits, arugula, onion, and basil in a large bowl. Toss with the vinaigrette and serve.

○ ○ ○ ○ ○ ○
A lovely little salad created by my friend John Willoughby.
○ ○ ○ ○ ○ ○ ○

Other greens to use:

Cress, dandelion, mizuna, or very young kale or collards. A mixture of any of these is also excellent.

Watercress and Sesame Salad

About 4 cups fresh water-cress, trimmed, washed, and dried according to directions on pages 6-8

2 tablespoons rice or wine vinegar

2 tablespoons soy sauce

1/2 teaspoon sugar

1/4 teaspoon cayenne, or to taste

1 teaspoon sesame oil

Salt to taste

2 tablespoons sesame seeds, toasted in a pan over medium heat until they begin to pop and change color

Makes 4 servings

Time: 10 minutes

Chop the watercress coarsely and place in a bowl. Mix together the vinegar, soy sauce, sugar, and cayenne, and dress the cress with this mixture. Toss; add the sesame oil and toss again. Taste and add salt if necessary. Garnish with the sesame seeds and serve.

Other greens to use:

Arugula or mizuna would be best, but you can make this recipe with any green you can eat raw.

Dandelion Greens with Peanuts and Tomatoes

4 cups young, tender
  dandelion greens, trimmed,
  washed, and dried according
  to the directions on pages 6-8
1 tablespoon peanut oil
1 teaspoon chile powder

1/2 cup roasted peanuts,
  with or without salt
Salt
1 cup chopped ripe tomatoes
The juice of 1 lime

Makes 4 servings
Time: 15 minutes

If the greens are very tender, chop them coarsely and add them to a bowl. If not, steam or parboil them (pages 8-9) for a minute or two, then rinse in cold water; dry.

Heat the peanut oil in a small saucepan over medium heat; add the chile powder and cook, stirring, until the chile powder darkens 30 to 60 seconds. Add the peanuts, toss, and cook, stirring constantly, for about a minute. Add salt if necessary. Toss together the dandelions, peanuts, and tomatoes. Taste and add more salt if necessary. Sprinkle the lime juice over all and serve.

Other greens to use:

Mizuna, young kale or collards, or young broccoli raab.

Chicken Salad with Cabbage and Mint

1 whole chicken breast, bone in or out

2 cups chicken broth or water

2 tablespoons fish sauce (*nuoc mam,* available in Asian markets)

1 small head Napa or white cabbage, cored and shredded

2 carrots, peeled and shredded

¾ cup mint, roughly chopped

Salt and freshly ground black pepper

½ teaspoon cayenne, or to taste

¼ cup lime juice

Makes 4 servings

Time: 30 minutes or less

Simmer the chicken breast in the stock or water; add 1 tablespoon of the fish sauce as it cooks. When the chicken is done, remove it from the bone if necessary and shred it; reserve the stock for another use.

Combine the shredded chicken with the cabbage, carrots, and ½ cup of the mint. Season with the salt, pepper, and cayenne. Dress with the remaining fish sauce and the lime juice; mince the remaining mint and use it to garnish the salad.

⊙ ⊙ ⊙ ⊙ ⊙ ⊙

A variation on a Vietnamese standard, taught to me by my friend Binh Duong.

⊙ ⊙ ⊙ ⊙ ⊙ ⊙ ⊙

Other greens to use:

Cabbages are best for this recipe, but you can use one of the sturdier lettuces, such as romaine, if you like.

Endives, Scallions, and Mint with Yogurt Dressing

4 Belgian endives, trimmed
  and separated into leaves
4 fresh scallions, trimmed and
  minced
2 cups (two 8-ounce
  containers) yogurt

1 small clove garlic, minced
Salt and freshly ground black
  pepper
$^1/_4$ cup minced fresh mint
Several mint leaves, for garnish

Makes 4 servings
Time: 15 minutes

Lay the endives out in a pretty pattern on a serving platter; sprinkle the scallions over them. Mix together the yogurt, garlic, salt, pepper, and mint; dress the endive with this mixture, garnish with mint, and serve.

Other greens to use:

Nothing will look as pretty as Belgian endive, but you could use any chicory, endive, or radicchio.

The Best and Simplest Green Salad

3 cups assorted small greens
and flowers, the widest
assortment you can find
(see page 30, mesclun),
trimmed, washed, and dried
according to the directions
on pages 6-8
1/4 to 1/3 cup extra virgin olive
or walnut oil

1 or 2 tablespoons authentic
balsamic vinegar or sherry
vinegar
Salt
Freshly ground black pepper,
optional

Makes 2 servings
Time: 5 minutes

Place the greens in a bowl and drizzle them with oil, vinegar, and a pinch of salt. Toss and taste. Correct seasoning, add
black pepper if desired, and serve immediately.

⊙ ⊙ ⊙ ⊙ ⊙ ⊙ ⊙

*The difference between an
average salad and a great one
takes no more than the ability to
procure great ingredients and
the patience to combine them. I
had my first really good salad in
the Alps in 1976, and my second
five years later, when I first
started growing greens. Now
you can buy surprisingly good
mesclun mixes in the supermarket; combine them with top
quality oil and vinegar, a dash
of salt, and forget about eating
dessert.*

⊙ ⊙ ⊙ ⊙ ⊙ ⊙ ⊙

Some Green Salad Variations

Almost any combination of greens can be used to make a salad, and you don't have to get fussy about dressings, either. Wash, trim, and dry all greens according to the directions on pages 6-8, and if you have any fresh herbs or edible flowers, throw them in as well, always judiciously. Here are some ideas. Most are just fine dressed with lemon juice or vinegar, olive oil, and salt and fresh pepper, all to taste; in a few instances I've noted a preference for a different dressing, but suit yourself.

Makes 4 servings

Time: 15 minutes

⊙ ⊙ ⊙ ⊙ ⊙ ⊙ ⊙

About 2 cups arugula, trimmed, washed, and dried according to the directions on pages 6-8

About 2 cups young dandelion greens, trimmed, washed, and dried according to the directions on pages 6-8

A few pieces of chopped ham

3 or 4 shallots, peeled and minced

⊙ ⊙ ⊙ ⊙ ⊙ ⊙ ⊙

1 pound cabbage, cored and shredded

1 cup chopped tomato

5 scallions, trimmed and finely minced

½ cup minced parsley

¼ cup minced mint

⊙ ⊙ ⊙ ⊙ ⊙ ⊙ ⊙

1 pound cabbage, cored and shredded

5 scallions, trimmed and finely minced

2 carrots, peeled and shredded

About 4 cups any mild lettuce (Boston, romaine, etc.), trimmed, washed, and dried according to the directions on pages 6-8

1 cup young dandelion greens

3 or 4 radishes, washed and sliced

¼ cup minced mint or parsley

Some pieces of feta cheese

⊙ ⊙ ⊙ ⊙ ⊙ ⊙ ⊙

About 2 cups watercress, trimmed, washed, and dried according to the directions on pages 6-8

About 3 cups chopped Belgian endive

½ cup hazelnuts, toasted in a dry skillet over a medium flame until fragrant

⊙ ⊙ ⊙ ⊙ ⊙ ⊙ ⊙

About 4 cups arugula, trimmed, washed, and dried according to the directions on pages 6-8

1 cup top-quality brine-cured olives, pitted

A crumbling of blue cheese

○ ○ ○ ○ ○ ○ ○

5 to 6 cups mesclun, trimmed, washed, and dried according to the directions on pages 6-8

2 ounces soft goat cheese, at room temperature, cut into quarters

4 Garlic Croutons (page 91), freshly made, still warm, and not crumbled

○ ○ ○ ○ ○ ○ ○

About 4 cups watercress, trimmed, washed, and dried according to the directions on pages 6-8

About 2 cups peeled, sliced ripe pears

$\frac{1}{2}$ cup walnuts

○ ○ ○ ○ ○ ○ ○

About 2 cups escarole, chicory, or frisee, trimmed, washed, and dried according to the directions on pages 6-8

About 2 cups watercress or arugula, trimmed, washed, and dried according to the directions on pages 6-8

2 or 3 perfectly ripe tomatoes, cut in half, seeds shaken out, and minced

○ ○ ○ ○ ○ ○ ○

2 cups bitter greens, such as arugula or watercress, trimmed, washed, and dried according to the directions on pages 6-8

2 cups tender greens, such as Boston lettuce or mâche, trimmed, washed, and dried according to the directions on pages 6-8

2 cups Belgian endive, cut into rounds

1 crisp apple, peeled, cored, and diced

$\frac{1}{2}$ cup walnuts

○ ○ ○ ○ ○ ○ ○

1 head romaine lettuce, trimmed, washed, and dried according to the directions on pages 6-8

1 large or 2 small grapefruit, sectioned

2 tablespoons sunflower seeds, toasted in a dry skillet over a medium flame until fragrant

○ ○ ○ ○ ○ ○ ○

4 Belgian endive, cut into rounds

4 oranges, sectioned

1 cup arugula, trimmed, washed, and dried according to the directions on pages 6-8

$\frac{1}{2}$ cup pecans

○ ○ ○ ○ ○ ○ ○

1 cup dulse (page 36), soaked briefly in water, squeezed dry, and cut up

2 cups arugula or watercress, trimmed, washed, and dried according to the directions on pages 6-8

1 minced shallot

○ ○ ○ ○ ○ ○ ○

1 cup trimmed, thinly sliced celery

1 cup trimmed, thinly sliced fresh fennel

3 cups mixed mild lettuces, such as Boston, romaine, or red-leaf, trimmed, washed, and dried according to the directions on pages 6-8

A few very thin slices of Parmesan, crumbled

Warm Salad of Mâche and Scallops

2 tablespoons fresh lemon
  juice
2½ tablespoons peanut oil
1 tablespoon minced shallot
Salt and freshly ground
  black pepper

1 pound sea scallops, cut in
  half horizontally
6 cups mâche, trimmed,
  washed, and dried according
  to the directions on pages 6-8

Makes 4 servings
Time: About 15 minutes

In a small bowl, whisk together the lemon juice, 1½ tablespoons of the oil, the shallot, and 1 tablespoon of water. Season with salt and pepper.

Heat the remaining tablespoon of the oil in a 12-inch nonstick skillet over high heat. Add the scallops and sear until golden, 2 to 3 minutes per side.

In a large bowl, toss the mâche with half the dressing. Divide the salad among 4 plates, arrange the scallops over the salad, and drizzle the remaining dressing over them. Serve immediately.

Variation

Warm Salad of Mâche and Beets: Steam ½ pound beets until tender; cool a little and peel. Cut into thick slices. Toss the mâche with half the dressing, divide it among 4 plates, top with the beets, and drizzle the remaining dressing over all.

Other greens to use:

You need supreme tenderness here; that's why mâche is so perfect. Baby lettuces or a fine mesclun mixture will do nicely.

◎ ◎ ◎ ◎ ◎ ◎

This is far from a traditional Breton salad; nevertheless, I first had it in the restaurant of Michel St. Cast, which is in the lovely little fishing town of Cancale. This quick little salad can take a variety of forms; see the variation.

◎ ◎ ◎ ◎ ◎ ◎

Sorrel Salad with Hard-cooked Eggs

2 large to extra-large eggs
2 cups tender, mild lettuce,
  such as Boston, trimmed,
  washed, and dried according
  to the directions on pages 6-8

4 cups sorrel, trimmed,
  washed, and dried according
  to the directions on pages 6-8
Creamy Vinaigrette
  (page 96)

Makes 4 servings
Time: 20 minutes

Poke a tiny hole in the broad end of each of the eggs with a pin or a needle (this will keep the egg from cracking as it cools). Place the eggs in a small pot of water, bring the water to a simmer, and cook gently for 12 minutes. Leave the eggs in the pot and run them under cold water to chill.

Meanwhile, toss the lettuce and the sorrel together in a large bowl. Peel the eggs and chop coarsely. Toss the eggs and dressing with the greens. Serve immediately.

⊚ ⊚ ⊚ ⊚ ⊚ ⊚

This is a rich, old-fashioned salad, full of flavor.

⊚ ⊚ ⊚ ⊚ ⊚ ⊚ ⊚

Other greens to use:

Nothing tastes like sorrel. If you use arugula or cress, equally distinctive but quite dissimilar, you will want a different vinaigrette as well.

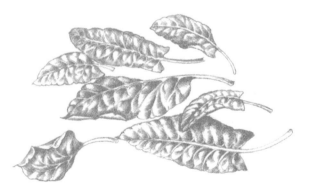

Mesclun with Goat Cheese and Garlic Croutons

5 to 6 cups mesclun, trimmed, washed, and dried according to the directions on pages 6-8

4 Garlic Croutons (recipe follows) made without cubing the bread and still warm

Basic Vinaigrette (page 95)

Makes 4 servings

Time: About 20 minutes

Divide the mesclun among 4 plates. Spread the croutons with the goat cheese, and top each portion of greens with a crouton. Dress lightly with the vinaigrette and serve.

Other greens to use:

Any mixture of tender greens you like will work here.

Garlic Croutons

4 tablespoons fruity extra
  virgin olive oil
4 cloves garlic, peeled

4 thick slices peasant bread,
  cut into cubes
Salt

Makes 4
Time: About 10 to 15 minutes

Warm the olive oil in a flat-bottomed skillet over medium-low heat; add the garlic and simmer it in the oil, turning occasionally, until it is lightly browned. Remove the garlic and reserve it for another use or toss it in the salad (you will find it to be very mild). Brown the bread lightly on both sides in the oil; remove and sprinkle it lightly with salt. Cool and use in any salad.

Variation

Whole croutons: There are times (see Mesclun with Goat Cheese and Garlic Croutons) when you will want whole slices of bread rather than cubes. Simply sauté the bread in the seasoned oil, turning once, until both sides are nicely browned.

○ ○ ○ ○ ○ ○ ○

There are an infinite number of ways to make crispy garlicky croutons for salad, but they basically fall into two categories. Those with fat and those without. To make those without, grill or broil a couple of thick slices of good peasant bread and rub them with a couple of cloves of cut garlic. To make those with, brush the bread with olive oil before grilling, or follow this recipe, which I believe is the ultimate.

○ ○ ○ ○ ○ ○ ○

Bitter Greens with Bacon

2 tablespoons olive oil

About ¹/₂ pound of the best-quality slab bacon you can find, cut into ¹/₂-inch cubes

1 tablespoon chopped shallot

4 cups dandelions, arugula, cress, chicory, escarole, or a combination, trimmed, washed, and dried according to the directions on pages 6-8

About ¹/₄ cup top-quality wine vinegar

1 teaspoon Dijon-style mustard

Salt and freshly ground black pepper

Makes 4 servings

Time: About 30 minutes

Warm the olive oil over medium heat in a skillet; add the bacon and cook slowly until it is crisp all over but not burnt or dried out. Add the shallot and cook a few moments longer, until the shallot softens. Keep the bacon warm in the skillet.

Heat a salad bowl by filling it with hot water and letting it sit for a minute or so. Dry it and toss in the greens. Add the vinegar and mustard to the skillet, and bring just to a boil, stirring. Pour the liquid and the bacon over the greens, season to taste (it shouldn't need much salt), and serve immediately.

◦ ◦ ◦ ◦ ◦ ◦

With good-quality bacon, this is one of the greatest food combinations ever. Must be served warm.

◦ ◦ ◦ ◦ ◦ ◦

Variation

With Boiled Potatoes: Simmer about a pound of waxy potatoes in salted water until tender; peel and cut into ¹/₂-inch chunks. Increase the quantity of oil, vinegar, and mustard slightly. Toss the potatoes with the greens just before topping with the dressing.

Cold Cooked Greens, Greek Style

1 to 2 pounds leafy greens,
  such as spinach, dandelion,
  chard, beet, mustard, etc.
Several tablespoons of
  olive oil

Salt and freshly ground
  black pepper
2 lemons, cut in half

Makes 4 servings
Time: 20 minutes

Parboil the greens (pages 8-9) in salted water until tender, just a minute or two for spinach, somewhat longer for tougher greens; drain them well and cool them quickly by running them under cold water. Squeeze them dry and chop; sprinkle with olive oil, salt, and pepper, and serve with lemon halves.

⊙ ⊙ ⊙ ⊙ ⊙ ⊙ ⊙

Hardly a recipe, this technique is useful year-round, but especially in the summer, when you can use it with wild and garden greens as well as store-bought ones.

⊙ ⊙ ⊙ ⊙ ⊙ ⊙ ⊙

Napa Cabbage with Sesame Vinaigrette

1/4 cup sesame oil

1/4 cup olive oil

1/4 cup lime juice (2 limes)

2 tablespoons rice vinegar

2 tablespoons soy sauce

1 teaspoon sugar

1 teaspoon minced fresh jalapeño, or other hot chile, or cayenne to taste

Salt and freshly ground black pepper

1 small head Napa cabbage, about 1 pound

1 carrot, peeled and thinly sliced

2 tablespoons minced fresh mint

1/2 cup bean sprouts, optional

Makes 4 servings

Time: 15 minutes

Combine the first 8 ingredients and whisk to blend. Core and shred the cabbage, toss with the remaining ingredients. Top with the dressing and serve.

Other greens to use:

Green or red cabbage, or a combination.

○ ○ ○ ○ ○ ○ ○

My friend Chris Schlesinger serves this with grilled shrimp at his Cambridge restaurant, the East Coast Grill, and that's a great idea. But I like this simple little salad by itself.

○ ○ ○ ○ ○ ○ ○

Basic Vinaigrette

1 tablespoon vinegar—preferably sherry, but good red or white wine, champagne, or balsamic will do

½ teaspoon salt, or more to taste

2½ tablespoons olive oil, preferably high-quality extra virgin (you may want 3 tablespoons oil, depending on the vinegar)

½ teaspoon Dijon mustard
1 teaspoon minced shallots
Freshly ground pepper to taste

Enough to dress a salad for 2

Time: 5 minutes

Briefly mix the vinegar and salt with an immersion blender, food processor or blender, or whisk. Slowly add the oil in a stream (drop by drop if whisking) until an emulsion forms. Add the remaining oil faster, but still in a stream. Taste to adjust salt and add more oil if needed. Add mustard, shallots, and pepper to taste.

Emulsified vinaigrettes are only important if you care. Sometimes that extra creaminess is nice (and an emulsion blender works brilliantly). But usually it doesn't matter much; I just toss everything in a bowl and whisk it for 30 seconds or so.

Creamy Vinaigrette

1 small shallot, minced
Salt and freshly ground
  black pepper
1 rounded teaspoon Dijon
  mustard

½ cup fruity extra virgin
  olive oil
About ¼ cup top-quality
  wine vinegar
¼ cup heavy cream

Makes about 1 cup, enough to dress at least
6 to 8 cups of greens
Time: 5 minutes

In a small bowl, mix together the shallot, salt, pepper, and mustard. Add the olive oil and whisk well with a fork; add most of the vinegar and the cream and whisk again. Taste for seasoning and add salt, pepper, mustard, or vinegar as needed. Use immediately.

⊙ ⊙ ⊙ ⊙ ⊙ ⊙ ⊙

The secret ingredient in this creamy vinaigrette?—Cream. Don't cringe—there isn't that much, and the addition is worth it.

⊙ ⊙ ⊙ ⊙ ⊙ ⊙ ⊙

Walnut Oil Vinaigrette

1 tablespoon sherry or good
  red wine vinegar
½ teaspoon salt

2 tablespoons walnut oil
Freshly ground pepper
  to taste

Makes about a quarter cup, enough for a
salad for 1 or 2
Time: 5 minutes

Briefly mix the vinegar and salt with an immersion blender, food processor or blender, or whisk. Slowly add the oil in a stream (drop by drop if whisking) until an emulsion forms. Add the remaining oil faster, but still in a stream. Taste to adjust salt and add more oil if needed. Add the mustard, shallots, and pepper to taste.

⊙ ⊙ ⊙ ⊙ ⊙ ⊙ ⊙

The strong, wonderful flavor of walnut oil means you need less in a dressing. This dressing illustrates the point that the ratio of oil to vinegar in dressings is as much a function of taste as of chemistry.

⊙ ⊙ ⊙ ⊙ ⊙ ⊙ ⊙

Lemon Vinaigrette

¾ teaspoon lemon zest
½ teaspoon salt
2 tablespoons lemon juice

3 to 4 tablespoons olive oil,
preferably extra virgin

Mix the zest, salt, and juice briefly with an immersion blender, food processor or blender, or whisk. Slowly add the oil in a stream (drop by drop if whisking) until an emulsion forms. Add the remaining oil faster, but still in a stream. Taste to adjust the salt and add more oil if needed. Let sit to develop the flavor; if you are serving this immediately, you may want to add a bit more lemon juice to sharpen the flavor.

○ ○ ○ ○ ○ ○

An all-purpose vinaigrette, especially wonderful for salads or warm dishes that contain fish.

○ ○ ○ ○ ○ ○

Variations

Lemon-thyme vinaigrette: Add ½ teaspoon finely minced fresh thyme to the vinaigrette.

Lemon-dill vinaigrette: Add 2 teaspoons finely minced dill; this must sit for the flavor to develop.

Lemon-tarragon: Add ½ teaspoon dried tarragon to the vinaigrette; or for a fuller flavor, add ½ teaspoon Dijon mustard to the vinegar and reduce the salt to ¼ teaspoon; then add ½ teaspoon dried tarragon to the completed vinaigrette.

Lemon-onion: Add 1 small onion, peeled and minced; let sit for a while before serving.

Orange Vinaigrette

¾ teaspoon orange zest
¼ teaspoon salt

2 tablespoons orange juice
3 tablespoons olive oil

Makes about ⅓ cup
Time: About 5 minutes

Follow the method for lemon vinaigrette, page 97.

◉ ◉ ◉ ◉ ◉ ◉

A good vinaigrette for salads with chicken.

◉ ◉ ◉ ◉ ◉ ◉

Variation

Orange-thyme vinaigrette: Add ½ to 1 teaspoon finely minced fresh thyme.

Lime Vinaigrette

½ teaspoon lime zest
¼ teaspoon salt

2 tablespoons juice
4 tablespoons olive oil

Makes ⅓ cup
Time: About 5 minutes

Follow the method for lemon vinaigrette. The flavor gets considerably sharper as it sits.

◉ ◉ ◉ ◉ ◉ ◉

Great for spicy salads or for those with beef, lamb, or pork.

◉ ◉ ◉ ◉ ◉ ◉

Nutty Vinaigrette

$^1\!/_2$ cup almonds, hazelnuts,
   pine nuts, pecans, or walnuts
1 small clove garlic, peeled
$^1\!/_4$ cup sherry or top-quality
   wine vinegar

Salt and freshly ground black
   pepper
$^3\!/_4$ cup olive oil

Makes about 1 cup

Time: 10 minutes

Toast the nuts in a dry skillet over medium heat, shaking almost constantly, until fragrant. Place the nuts and garlic in the container of a blender or small food processor and pulverize. Add the vinegar, salt, and pepper, then the oil a bit at a time. The mixture will become creamy and quite thick. Taste to make sure the acid balance pleases you and add more vinegar if you like; if the taste is good but the mixture is too thick, add warm water, a bit at a time.

○ ○ ○ ○ ○ ○

You can use almost any nut at all for this dressing; it's best to peel those such as almonds and hazelnuts.

○ ○ ○ ○ ○ ○

Anchovy-Caper Vinaigrette

4 anchovy fillets, with a bit of
   their oil
1 teaspoon capers, with a bit
   of their brine
About $^3\!/_4$ cup fruity extra
   virgin olive oil
About $^1\!/_4$ cup sherry or top-
   quality wine vinegar

1 teaspoon Dijon-style
   mustard
Salt and freshly ground
   black pepper
1 tablespoon minced
   fresh parsley

Makes about 1 cup

Time: 10 minutes

Mince the anchovy fillets and mix them with their oil, the capers and their brine, and all the remaining ingredients except for the parsley. Taste and correct seasoning if necessary. Add parsley just before serving.

○ ○ ○ ○ ○ ○

A pungent dressing, not for the faint of heart. Use on flavorful greens.

○ ○ ○ ○ ○ ○

Vinaigrette in the Style of Mayonnaise

1 egg
1 teaspoon Dijon mustard
1 teaspoon minced shallot
¼ cup sherry or top-quality
  wine vinegar

¾ cup olive, walnut, or
  hazelnut oil
Salt and freshly ground black
  pepper

Makes about 1 cup
Time: 10 minutes

Break the egg into a small bowl and beat with the mustard, shallot, and vinegar. Drizzle in the oil, a little at a time, beating constantly with a fork or wire whisk. When the mixture is as thick as heavy cream, add salt and pepper to taste.

◦ ◦ ◦ ◦ ◦ ◦ ◦

This is something of a cross between vinaigrette and mayonnaise, more vinegar-y and much thinner than the latter but much creamier than most vinaigrettes. If the thought of raw eggs worries you, substitute an equivalent amount of a pasteurized egg substitute such as Egg Beaters.

◦ ◦ ◦ ◦ ◦ ◦ ◦

Tahini Dressing

1 clove garlic
1 teaspoon salt
1 cup tahini
½ cup water

½ cup freshly squeezed
  lemon juice
Paprika or cumin for garnish

Makes about 2 cups
Time: 10 minutes

Use a mortar and pestle or small food processor to make the garlic and salt into a paste. Add the tahini; the mixture will be very thick. Add the water, followed by the lemon juice. If the mixture is thicker than you'd like, add more water. Check for salt and serve, topped with a little paprika or cumin.

Side Dishes

Chard with Garlic, Pine Nuts, and Currants

2 pounds Swiss chard, washed
  and trimmed according to
  the directions on pages 6-8
2 tablespoons olive oil
1 tablespoon minced garlic
1/2 cup pignoli (pine nuts)

1/2 cup currants, soaked in
  warm water for about 10
  minutes, drained
Salt and freshly ground black
  pepper to taste

Makes 4 servings
Time: 20 minutes

Cut the chard stems into 1- to 2-inch lengths, then coarsely chop the leaves. Steam or parboil the stems (pages 8-9) until they are almost tender, then add the chopped leaves. Continue to cook until both the stems and leaves are quite tender, another couple of minutes. Drain, and when the chard is cool enough, squeeze dry.

Heat the oil over medium-low heat in a 10- or 12-inch skillet and add the garlic; cook just until the garlic begins to color, a couple of minutes. Add the pignolis and cook another minute, stirring, then add the chard, currants, and salt and pepper; cook, stirring, for about 2 minutes. Serve hot or at room temperature.

○ ○ ○ ○ ○ ○

A sweet dish, wonderful as an accompaniment to savory meats; thin it with a little more olive oil and some of the chard cooking water to make a good pasta sauce.

○ ○ ○ ○ ○ ○

Other greens to use:

Spinach is often served with pine nuts and currants, and it's wonderful that way; I like young, not-too-bitter dandelion greens, too.

Gingered Cabbage

2 tablespoons peanut or
  olive oil
1 small head Savoy cabbage,
  about 1¹/₂ pounds, cored,
  shredded, and chopped
1 tablespoon minced garlic
Salt and freshly ground black
  pepper to taste

1 tablespoon peeled and
  minced ginger
Juice of 1 lemon
Minced fresh parsley or
  cilantro for garnish

Makes 4 servings
Time: 30 minutes

Heat the oil in a large skillet over medium-high heat, and
sauté the cabbage, stirring occasionally. When it is limp but not
mushy, after about 10 minutes, add the garlic, salt, and pepper,
and cook another 2 minutes, stirring. Add the ginger, cook another minute, and remove to a platter. Drizzle with the lemon
juice, sprinkle with the parsley or cilantro, and serve.

Other greens to use:

Any cabbage or chard.

⊚ ⊚ ⊚ ⊚ ⊚ ⊚

*What makes cabbage so great
with ginger? I don't know, but
there isn't a variety—green,
Savoy, Red, Chinese, or
otherwise—that doesn't take to
this treatment.*

⊚ ⊚ ⊚ ⊚ ⊚ ⊚

Lightly, Quickly Pickled Cabbage

6 cups red or green cabbage,
   cored and shredded into
   ⅛- to ¼-inch slices
1 tablespoon salt
1 red onion

1 cucumber
1 teaspoon caraway seeds
2 tablespoons rice or wine
   vinegar

Makes 4 to 6 servings
Time: 45 minutes

Toss the cabbage in a colander with the salt. Peel and slice the red onion; separate it into rings and toss with the cabbage. Peel the cucumber if you like and cut it in half, lenthwise. If there are a lot of seeds, scoop them out with a spoon. Slice the cucumber thinly and mix it with the cabbage and onion. Lay a plate over the vegetable mixture while it is still in the colander and weight the plate with whatever is handy: a few cans, some rocks, your teakettle filled with water, whatever. Let rest for about 30 minutes to an hour.

Rinse the mixture, add the vinegar, and serve. This will keep refrigerated quite nicely for a day or two.

Variation

Pickled Cabbage, Chinese Style: Toss the cabbage with the salt and press with no other ingredients. An hour later, toss with 1 teaspoon crushed Sechuan peppercorns, 1 tablespoon sherry, 1 tablespoon soy sauce, and 1 teaspoon sesame oil. Marinate for an hour, and serve or refrigerate. This will keep a day or two.

Other greens to use:

Cabbage is best; bok choi or chard will also work. See Pickled Bok Choi, page 106.

Toasted Nori with Salt

4 sheets nori (laver)
4 teaspoons sesame oil
Salt

Heat a 12-inch non-stick skillet over medium heat. Brush one sheet of nori, both sides, with a teaspoon of sesame oil. Toast it for about 30 to 60 seconds in the skillet; turn and repeat. Remove the sheet and repeat the process three more times. As each sheet comes out of the skillet, sprinkle it with salt and cut it (with a scissors; it's the easiest way) into quarters. Stack the quarters on top of one another. Serve as a snack or on top of a bed of rice as a side dish.

Makes 4 servings
Time: 10 minutes

This simple, slightly bizarre—to Western palates at least—and surprisingly flavorful concoction is a wonderful introduction to the joys of sea vegetables. I love it as a snack.

Pickled Bok Choi

1 head bok choi,
  about 1½ pounds
5 whole scallions, chopped up
5 cloves of garlic, peeled and
  roughly chopped
2 or 3 fresh jalapeños or
  dried red chiles, minced, or
  to taste

1 tablespoon sugar
2 tablespoons salt
1 tablespoon minced fresh
  ginger
2 tablespoons water

Makes 4 to 8 servings as a side dish
Time: 15 minutes of work, 2 to 3 days of waiting

Chop the bok choi coarsely into 1- to 2-inch pieces. Place it in a large bowl, add the remaining ingredients, and toss. Place in a jar (or leave in the bowl) and cover tightly. Keep at room temperature for a day, then refrigerate. It will be ready to eat after 2 or 3 days and will keep for weeks.

Other greens to use:

Broccoli raab, any cabbage, chard, or mustard or turnip greens.

There are more ways to preserve cabbage than making sauerkraut, and many of them originated in Asia. Here's a simple version that I like a lot; once made, it's an instant, super-savory side dish.

Spinach in Coconut Milk

1 cup dried,
  unsweetened coconut
1 cup boiling water
1 tablespoon peanut or
  vegetable oil
1 teaspoon minced
  fresh ginger
1 teaspoon minced garlic

1 jalapeño, stemmed, seeded,
  and deveined, or 1 dried red
  chile pepper
Salt and freshly ground
  black pepper to taste
1 pound spinach, washed
  according to the directions
  on page 39

Makes 4 servings
Time: 20 minutes

Place the coconut in a blender and cover it with 1 cup boiling water. Cover the blender, and holding the top on with a folded towel to reduce the possibilities of scalding, blend for 20 seconds or so. Let the mixture sit for a few minutes, then strain, pressing to extract as much liquid as possible.

Heat the peanut oil in a large skillet over medium heat and add the ginger and garlic. Cook, stirring, until the garlic begins to color. Add the coconut milk and the jalapeño or chile and bring to a boil; lower the heat, add salt and pepper, and taste. Chop the spinach coarsely and simmer it in the liquid about five minutes. Raise the heat to high and boil off any excess liquid, stirring occasionally. Serve immediately.

Creamed spinach without the cream but with a ton of flavor.

Other greens to use:

Chard.

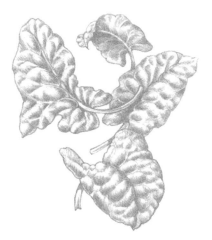

Mustard Greens Tossed with Oyster Sauce and Basil

2 tablespoons peanut oil

2 jalapeños, stemmed, seeded, and deveined, or 2 dried red chiles, or to taste

1 tablespoon minced garlic

1½ pounds mustard greens, washed and trimmed according to the directions on pages 6-8 and coarsely chopped

1 tablespoon oyster sauce (available in Asian markets)

1 tablespoon soy sauce

¼ cup chopped fresh basil

Salt and freshly ground black pepper to taste

Makes 4 servings
Time: 10 minutes

Heat the peanut oil in a large skillet or wok over medium-high heat. Add the peppers and garlic and toss until the garlic begins to color, about 30 seconds. Add the greens and cook over high heat, stirring frequently, until they wilt and become tender, about 3 to 5 minutes. Add the oyster sauce and soy sauce and cook, stirring, about 30 seconds more. Add the basil, taste for seasoning, and serve, preferably over white rice.

⊚ ⊚ ⊚ ⊚ ⊚ ⊚

A spicy stir-fry you can throw together in minutes.

⊚ ⊚ ⊚ ⊚ ⊚ ⊚

Other greens to use:

Broccoli raab, collards, kale, turnips.

Sautéed Broccoli Raab with Curry

About 1½ pounds broccoli
  raab, washed and trimmed
  according to the directions
  on pages 6-8
Salt
2 tablespoons peanut or
  vegetable oil

1 teaspoon yellow
  mustard seeds
1 teaspoon cumin seeds
1 tablespoon minced garlic
1 tablespoon curry powder
1 tablespoon lemon juice

Makes 4 servings

Time: 20 minutes

Bring a pot of water to a boil. Trim the broccoli raab of thick, tough stems; peel the stems if they are thicker than a pencil. Cut the broccoli raab into 1- to 2-inch pieces. Salt the water and parboil (pages 8-9) the broccoli raab until it is bright green and crisp-tender, about 3 minutes.

Heat the oil in a wok or large skillet over medium heat. Add the mustard and cumin seeds and cover the pan for a few seconds (the mustard seeds will pop). Remove the cover, add the garlic and curry and cook, stirring, until the garlic colors and the curry becomes fragrant, about 2 minutes. Add the broccoli, raise the heat to high and cook, stirring, until the broccoli is coated with the spice mixture and is completely tender, a few minutes. Sprinkle with the lemon juice and serve immediately or at room temperature.

A fast curry that's great over rice and makes an ideal lunch.

Other greens to use:

Collards, kale, mustard, turnips.

Turnip Greens with Potatoes

2 tablespoons peanut or
vegetable oil
1 teaspoon minced garlic
1 teaspoon cumin
1/2 teaspoon turmeric
1 pound turnip greens,
washed according to the
directions on pages 6-7
2 small red potatoes, about
1/2 pound, washed well and
peeled if desired, cut into
1/2 inch dice

1/2 cup chicken or vegetable
stock or water
Salt and freshly ground black
pepper to taste
1 teaspoon rice or wine
vinegar

Makes 4 servings

Time: 30 minutes

Heat the oil in a large skillet over medium heat. Add the garlic and cook until it begins to color; add the remaining spice and cook, stirring, until the mixture is fragrant, about 1 minute. Add the turnip greens, the potatoes, and the stock or water, stir, cover, and reduce the heat to medium-low. Cook, checking and stirring every 3 or 4 minutes, until the potato is tender, 10 to 15 minutes. Raise the heat to high and boil off excess liquid, if any. Season to taste, drizzle with vinegar, and serve immediately.

Other greens to use:

Broccoli raab, collards, cress, dandelions, kale, mizuna, mustard.

○ ○ ○ ○ ○ ○

You can make this into a soup simply by adding more stock; if you do so, you might want to double the amount of potatoes and throw in a minced onion.

○ ○ ○ ○ ○ ○ ○

Sushi-Style Spinach

10 ounces spinach, cleaned,
  tough stems removed
½ cup sesame seeds
Salt to taste

1 teaspoon soy sauce
1 teaspoon dark sesame oil

Makes 4 servings
Time: 20 minutes

Bring a large pot of water to boil, and add salt. While you are waiting, toast the sesame seeds by heating them in a dry skillet over medium heat, shaking occasionally, until they begin to pop and color; place them in a small bowl.

When the water boils, cook the spinach until it wilts and the stems become tender, 30 seconds to 2 minutes. Remove it with a strainer or slotted spoon and immediately plunge it into a bowl of ice water; when it has cooled off, squeeze the excess water from it and chop it fine.

Sprinkle the spinach with a little salt and the soy sauce, and shape it into a 1-inch thick log (if you have a bamboo sushi-rolling mat, use this to achieve a perfect shape). Cut the log into 1-inch long slices; dip each end of each slice into the sesame seeds and arrange on a plate. Drizzle with the sesame oil. Serve immediately or refrigerate.

Other greens to use:

Dandelion or mizuna will work, but spinach is really the best.

○ ○ ○ ○ ○ ○ ○
This is really easy to do and very impressive. I've taught many of my friends how to do this, and it's become part of their entertaining repertoires.
○ ○ ○ ○ ○ ○ ○

Spinach with Walnuts, Anchovies, and Raisins

1 tablespoon olive oil
3 or 4 anchovy fillets, optional
2 large cloves garlic, peeled and slivered
¼ cup walnuts
¼ cup raisins

10 ounces to 1 pound spinach, cleaned, tough stems removed, well drained, and coarsely chopped
Salt and freshly ground black pepper to taste

Makes 4 servings
Time: 15 minutes

Heat the olive oil over medium heat in a 10- or 12-inch skillet, preferably non-stick, for about a minute. Add the anchovies and cook for about a minute, stirring with a wooden spoon and breaking them up. Add the garlic and walnuts, stir, and cook until the garlic colors a bit. Add the raisins, stir, and cook another 30 seconds. Add the spinach and cover. Cook 3 to 5 minutes, until the spinach has wilted. Uncover the skillet, raise the heat to medium high, and cook, stirring, until most of the liquid has evaporated; season to taste and serve hot or at room temperature.

Other greens to use:

Chard is excellent prepared this way.

⊙ ⊙ ⊙ ⊙ ⊙ ⊙

A traditional dish of the Mediterranean, especially Sicily. Like the chard recipe on page 103 (with garlic, pine nuts, currants), it can be thinned with a little water to make a pasta sauce.

⊙ ⊙ ⊙ ⊙ ⊙ ⊙

Spinach, Indian Style (Saag)

2 pounds spinach, washed
  and trimmed according to
  the directions on page 39
2 tablespoons peanut or
  vegetable oil
1 tablespoon minced garlic
1 tablespoon minced ginger
1 fresh jalapeño, stemmed,
  seeded, and deveined, or 1
  or 2 dried red chiles

1 teaspoon good curry
  powder
1/4 cup water
Salt and freshly ground black
  pepper
1/2 cup heavy cream
1/4 cup minced fresh cilantro

Makes 4 to 8 servings
Time: About 35 minutes

Chop the spinach coarsely.

Heat the oil over medium-low heat in a steep-sided skillet
that can later be covered. Add the garlic, ginger, and chile and
cook, stirring, until the garlic begins to color. Add the curry powder and cook, stirring, for another minute or so. Add the spinach,
toss, and cover. Cook 3 to 5 minutes, until the spinach wilts.

Check that the mixture isn't too dry; if it is, add the water.
Recover the skillet, reduce the heat to low and cook, stirring occasionally, for about 15 minutes, until the spinach is very soft and
dark.

Uncover, add salt and pepper to taste, and stir in the cream.
Cover and cook over the lowest heat possible for another 5 to 10
minutes, stirring once or twice. Garnish with the fresh cilantro
and serve immediately.

⊙ ⊙ ⊙ ⊙ ⊙ ⊙
*This is often served with cubes
of the cheese known as paneer;
I always felt that the cheese got
in the way of this fantastic
preparation.*
⊙ ⊙ ⊙ ⊙ ⊙ ⊙

Sautéed Young Collards with Cumin and Tangerine

1 pound collards, washed and trimmed according to the directions on pages 6-8

2 tablespoons peanut or vegetable oil

1 tablespoon cumin

¼ teaspoon cayenne, optional

Salt and freshly ground black pepper

1 teaspoon freshly grated tangerine rind (wash the tangerine first)

½ cup freshly squeezed tangerine juice

Makes 4 servings

Time: 30 minutes

Remove any thick stems from the collards, chop them roughly, and parboil them briefly (pages 8-9), until they are beginning to become tender, about 5 minutes; rinse under cold water and squeeze dry.

Heat a 12-inch non-stick skillet over medium-high heat and add the oil. Add the cumin and cayenne and stir for a few seconds; add the collards and season to taste. Cook for a few minutes, stirring occasionally, until the collards are tender and fragrant.

Add the tangerine rind and juice, stir, raise the heat to high for 30 seconds, and serve.

Other greens to use:

Kale, mustard.

⊙ ⊙ ⊙ ⊙ ⊙ ⊙ ⊙

A midwinter dish that will warm your bones; if you can't get young, tender collards use spinach, kale, or chard. Just make sure none of the stems are thicker than an eighth of an inch or so.

⊙ ⊙ ⊙ ⊙ ⊙ ⊙ ⊙

Dandelion with Toasted Garlic and Lemon

2 tablespoons olive oil

2 tablespoons butter
(or use all olive oil)

5 to 10 cloves garlic, peeled
and cut into thin slices

1 ½ pounds dandelion
greens, washed and
trimmed according to the
directions on pages 6-8;
spun or patted dry

Salt and freshly ground
black pepper

One lemon, cut into quarters

Makes 4 servings

Time: 15 minutes

Heat the oil and butter together, over medium heat, in a 10- or 12-inch non-stick skillet. When the butter foam subsides, toss in the garlic and cook, stirring frequently, until it becomes light brown and crunchy; this will take 5 minutes or so. Do not let the garlic burn. Remove it from the skillet with a slotted spoon.

Chop the dandelion greens coarsely, raise the heat to high, and sauté the greens until they are tender but not mushy, about 5 minutes. Season to taste and remove to a bowl; if any pan drippings remain, pour them over the greens. Top with the toasted garlic and serve with the lemon wedges.

Other greens to use:

Try watercress, mizuna, or young broccoli raab, collards, kale, mustard, or turnips. If the greens are older, parboil them first.

◎ ◎ ◎ ◎ ◎ ◎ ◎

Although this is a close relation of the broccoli raab recipe on page 121 (Broccoli Raab, New Haven Style), it demonstrates yet another character of garlic, this one sweet and crunchy.

◎ ◎ ◎ ◎ ◎ ◎ ◎

Basic Bok Choi

1½ pounds bok choi washed and trimmed according to the directions on pages 6-8
2 tablespoons peanut oil
1 cup good chicken stock

Salt and freshly ground black pepper
1 teaspoon sesame oil, optional

Makes 4 servings
Time: About 30 minutes

If the bok choi stems are wide, cut them in half lengthwise; then cut them into 1- to 2-inch lengths (if they are narrow, just cut them into pieces). Heat the peanut oil in a wok or broad skillet over medium-high heat for 3 or 4 minutes; toss in the cabbage and cook, stirring, until it begins to brown, about 5 minutes. Add the stock, salt, and pepper, and cover; lower the heat and simmer for 5 to 10 minutes more, until the bok choi is soft and creamy. Remove the cover, boil off the excess liquid, check the seasoning, and serve. Drizzle with the sesame oil if you like.

Other greens to use:

The results will not be the same, but the technique can be used with any cabbage or dark green; older greens with thicker stems must be parboiled first.

⊙ ⊙ ⊙ ⊙ ⊙ ⊙ ⊙

Bok choi takes on an entirely different character when it is cooked for a long time: It becomes creamy and is unlike anything else. There's a soothing, comforting food quality about it, and you don't have to be Asian to appreciate it.

⊙ ⊙ ⊙ ⊙ ⊙ ⊙ ⊙

Sweet and Sour Chinese Cabbage

2 tablespoons peanut oil
1 red bell pepper, cored and
  cut into thin slices
1 medium to large onion,
  peeled and cut into rings
1 head bok choi, Napa, or
  other Chinese cabbage,
  washed and trimmed
  according to the directions
  on pages 6-8

2 tablespoons sugar
2 tablespoons rice or
  wine vinegar
1 tablespoon soy sauce
Salt

Makes 4 servings
Time: 15 minutes

Heat the peanut oil over medium-high heat in a wok or large skillet. When it shimmers, add the pepper, raise the heat to high, and stir-fry for 2 or 3 minutes, until it softens. Remove with a slotted spoon, leaving the heat on high. Add the onion and stir-fry until it softens, 2 to 3 minutes. Remove. Add the cabbage and toss until it softens and browns, 4 to 5 minutes. Return the pepper and the onion to the wok and continue to stir-fry, always over high heat, until the mixture is completely tender.

Stir in the sugar, vinegar, and soy sauce and cook for 30 seconds. Taste for seasonings—you may add more sugar or vinegar if you like—and salt if necessary. Serve immediately.

⊙ ⊙ ⊙ ⊙ ⊙ ⊙ ⊙

A very basic, quick recipe that you can make with any cabbage you find. Great with other stir-fries, of course, but equally good with a variety of spicy dishes.

⊙ ⊙ ⊙ ⊙ ⊙ ⊙ ⊙

Variation:

Chinese Cabbage with Black Mushrooms and Ginger: Soak 3 dried black or shiitake mushrooms in hot water until soft. After cooking the red pepper, add 1 teaspoon each minced garlic and ginger to remaining oil. Toss for 30 seconds, then add the cabbage. Trim and mince the mushrooms and mix them into the cabbage as it cooks. Complete the recipe as above.

Other greens to use:

Any cabbage or dark green; those with thicker stems must be parboiled (pages 8-9) until nearly tender before proceeding.

Spicy Cole Slaw

2 tablespoons Dijon mustard
2 tablespoons sherry or
  balsamic vinegar
½ cup olive, peanut, or
  vegetable oil
1 tablespoon sugar
6 cups shredded Napa, Savoy,
  green, or red cabbage

2 cups diced red pepper
1 cup diced scallion
Salt and freshly ground black
  pepper
¼ cup minced parsley

Makes about 2 quarts
Time: 20 minutes

Whisk together the mustard and vinegar; add the oil a little at a time, whisking all the while. Add the sugar and whisk to dissolve. Combine the cabbage, pepper, and scallion, and toss with the dressing. Season with salt and pepper and refrigerate until ready to serve (it's best to let this rest for an hour or so before serving to allow the flavors to mellow). Just before serving, toss with minced parsley.

Variation

Cole Slaw, Asian-style: Combine the cabbage, red pepper, and scallion as above. Toast a tablespoon of sesame seeds in a dry skillet over medium heat, shaking, until they color. Combine them with ½ cup rice vinegar, 1 teaspoon minced or grated ginger, 1 tablespoon sesame oil, 2 tablespoons peanut oil, and whisk thoroughly. Toss with the cabbage mixture and serve.

◎ ◎ ◎ ◎ ◎ ◎ ◎
Prettier and better tasting than the traditional bland, mayo-laced slaw. Add a few fennel or anise seeds if you like.
◎ ◎ ◎ ◎ ◎ ◎ ◎

Steamed and Sautéed Kale

1 pound kale, the younger the
  better
$\frac{1}{4}$ cup olive oil
$\frac{1}{4}$ cup garlic, peeled and
  thinly sliced (about 5 or 6
  cloves)

$\frac{1}{2}$ teaspoon red pepper flakes
$\frac{3}{4}$ teaspoon salt
Piece of lemon rind

If the stems are greater than $\frac{1}{4}$ inch in diameter, strip the leaves (pages 7-8) and discard the stems. Otherwise, cut the stems into 1-inch lengths and chop the leaves coarsely.

Place the olive oil in a large saucepan. Add the garlic, pepper flakes, and salt, and cook on high heat for about 1 minute. Meanwhile, wash the kale in cold water, lifting it out of the water and shaking it briefly to remove most of the water. Add it to the saucepan. (The water remaining on the kale is enough for the cooking process.) Cover and cook on high heat for approximately 4 to 5 minutes, until the kale is wilted and just tender but still a little firm.

Arrange the kale on a plate and decorate the center with a piece of lemon rind; serve immediately.

The dark color, distinct flavor, and crinkly texture of kale makes this simple preparation a winner.

Variation

Kale with Double Garlic: Add another teaspoon of minced garlic to the kale about a minute before it is done; it will cook just long enough to remove its harsh flavor but will still be bold and flavorful.

Other greens to use:

Broccoli raab, collards, dandelion, mustard, turnips.

Kale, Brazilian Style

1½ pounds young kale or
    collards
3 tablespoons olive or
    peanut oil

Salt and freshly ground
    pepper to taste
¼ to ⅓ cup freshly squeezed
    lemon juice, or vinegar

Wash the greens well, then dry them in a salad spinner and towel; no water should remain on the leaves. Roughly chop the greens. Meanwhile, heat a 12-inch skillet or wok over high heat until smoking. Add the oil to the skillet, let sit for a few seconds, then toss in the greens. Cook over high heat, stirring almost constantly, until they wilt, 3 to 5 minutes. Season with salt and pepper and add some lemon juice or vinegar. Taste and adjust the seasoning and serve immediately.

⊙ ⊙ ⊙ ⊙ ⊙ ⊙

It's best to use relatively small leaves for this dish, which cooks far too quickly to soften tough stems.

⊙ ⊙ ⊙ ⊙ ⊙ ⊙

Other greens to use:

Broccoli raab, chard, dandelions, collards, mustard, turnips; all should be quite young.

Broccoli Raab, New Haven Style

1 pound broccoli raab,
  washed and trimmed
  according to the instructions
  on pages 6-8
3 tablespoons olive oil
1 tablespoon minced garlic

½ teaspoon red pepper flakes,
  or to taste
Salt and freshly ground
  black pepper
Lemon quarters

Makes 2 to 4 servings
Time: 20 minutes

Cut off the tough ends of the broccoli raab; if the stems are thicker than a pencil, use a paring knife to peel away the tough coating. Heat a 10- or 12-inch non-stick skillet over medium-high heat. Add the broccoli raab and the oil. Cover and cook over medium heat until the broccoli raab begins to wilt, 4 or 5 minutes. Remove the cover, add the garlic and red pepper and sauté over medium-high heat until the broccoli raab is nice and tender but still bright green, another 3 to 4 minutes. Season with salt and pepper; serve hot or at room temperature, with lemon.

Other greens to use:

Again, this is among the most useful recipes in this book. I've used it successfully (varying cooking times according to the tenderness of the green) with almost every bitter cooking green in this book. Try kale, collards, spinach, dandelions, turnips, mustard (closely related to broccoli raab as noted on page 18), Savoy or Chinese cabbage, or anything else you don't know what to do with.

⊚ ⊚ ⊚ ⊚ ⊚ ⊚ ⊚

This is how we do broccoli raab in New Haven, where good broccoli raab is always in demand. It's a basic recipe, and one of the most important in this book.

⊚ ⊚ ⊚ ⊚ ⊚ ⊚ ⊚

Mustard Greens with 5-Spice Powder

1½ pounds mustard greens, washed and trimmed according to the directions on pages 6-8

2 tablespoons peanut oil

Salt and freshly ground black pepper to taste

1 teaspoon 5-spice powder

¼ cup mirin (Japanese sweet wine, available at Asian markets) or 1 tablespoon honey mixed with 2 tablespoons warm water

2 tablespoons soy sauce mixed with 2 tablespoons white wine or water

2 cloves garlic, minced

1 teaspoon sugar

Makes 4 servings

Time: 20 minutes

Cut off the tough ends of the mustard; if the stems are thicker than a pencil, use a paring knife to peel away the tough coating. Heat the oil in a 12-inch skillet, preferably non-stick, over medium-high heat. When the oil begins to smoke, add the mustard greens; raise the heat to high and stir, adding the salt and pepper, until the greens are bright green and glistening with the oil.

Sprinkle with the 5-spice powder and mirin, stir, cover, reduce heat to medium and cook for about 5 minutes, until the mustard is nearly tender. Remove the cover, raise the heat again, and add the soy sauce, garlic, and sugar. Cook, stirring frequently, until the greens are fully tender and the sauce has thickened. Serve immediately over white rice.

Sharp mustard greens are the perfect foil for the sweet, exotic flavor of 5-spice powder. You can serve this as a main course with rice; add a little meat if you like.

Other greens to use:

Broccoli raab.

Turnip Greens in Mustard Sauce

2 tablespoons olive oil

About 2 pounds turnip
greens, washed according to
the directions on pages 6-7

Salt and freshly ground
pepper to taste

1 cup light chicken stock,
white wine, water, or a
combination

2 teaspoons cornstarch

3 tablespoons strong
Dijon-style mustard

¼ cup chopped parsley

Makes 4 servings

Time: About 20 minutes

Heat the oil over medium heat in a non-stick skillet that can
later be covered. Add the greens, salt and pepper, and cook briskly,
stirring occasionally, until the greens begin to wilt. Add the stock,
cover, and simmer until the greens are tender, 10 minutes or so.

Remove the greens with a slotted spoon to a serving bowl;
keep warm. Mix the cornstarch into the mustard and stir the mixture into the pan juices. Cook over low heat until lightly thickened, a minute or two.

Pour the sauce over the greens, garnish with chopped parsley, and serve.

◎ ◎ ◎ ◎ ◎ ◎ ◎

*This rich, warm, wintry dish
has a classic French feel to it.
It's superb with roasted chicken
or turkey.*

◎ ◎ ◎ ◎ ◎ ◎ ◎

Other greens to use:

Young broccoli raab, dandelions, or mustard.

Steamed Beet Greens with Oregano

About 1½ pounds beet
  greens, washed and
  trimmed according to the
  directions on pages 6-8
¼ cup freshly squeezed
  lemon juice
¼ cup fruity olive oil

1 tablespoon fresh oregano or
  marjoram, minced, or
  1 teaspoon dried
Salt and freshly ground
  black pepper

Makes 4 servings
Time: 15 minutes

Steam the beet greens (page 8) just until tender. Rinse them under cool water, then press out the moisture as much as you can. Chop finely.

Whisk together the lemon juice, olive oil, and oregano or marjoram. Dress the beet greens with this mixture, season to taste; serve at room temperature.

◎ ◎ ◎ ◎ ◎ ◎ ◎

A recipe that demonstrates just how easy it is to combine a few common ingredients to make a great-tasting plate of greens.

◎ ◎ ◎ ◎ ◎ ◎ ◎

Other greens to use:

Chard.

Braised Cabbage with Wine

2 tablespoons olive oil, lard, rendered chicken fat, or butter

1 head cabbage, red or white, about 1½ pounds, cored and shredded

Salt and freshly ground black pepper

1 cup red wine

1 tablespoon brown sugar

1 tablespoon top quality wine vinegar

Makes 4 servings

Time: Less than 30 minutes

Heat the fat of your choice over medium heat in a 12-inch non-stick skillet that can later be covered. Add the cabbage and stir until it begins to brown, about 5 minutes. Add salt and pepper to taste, then the wine; let the wine bubble away for a few moments, then add the sugar and vinegar. Cover and simmer until tender, about 15 minutes. Check the seasoning—you can add more salt, pepper, sugar, or vinegar if you like—and serve.

Variations

Braised Cabbage with Buttered Bread Crumbs: Follow the original recipe. Top the cabbage with a cup of bread crumbs (preferably fresh), which have been sautéed briefly in 2 tablespoons of butter (or whichever fat you choose). Run under the broiler to brown before serving.

Cabbage Braised with Apples, Bacon, and Potatoes: Begin by sautéing ½ pound good quality bacon, cut into small dice, until crisp. Add the cabbage and 2 potatoes, peeled and cut into chunks; after the wine bubbles away, add 2 apples, peeled, cored, and cut into chunks (omit sugar). Finish as in original recipe.

⊙ ⊙ ⊙ ⊙ ⊙ ⊙ ⊙

You can braise any cabbage, red, white, bok choi, Savoy— they'll all be great. The following, a collection of recipes from northern Europe, are traditionally made with red or white cabbage. For variety, add some peeled, cored, and cut-up apples to the cabbage, along with a clove or two.

⊙ ⊙ ⊙ ⊙ ⊙ ⊙ ⊙

Braised Endive

1 tablespoon olive oil
8 Belgian endives, trimmed at the base, damaged leaves removed
$\frac{1}{4}$ cup minced ham, preferably proscuitto or other dry-cured ham

$\frac{1}{2}$ cup stock or water
Salt and freshly ground black pepper
1 teaspoon lemon juice or good vinegar

Makes 4 servings
Time: About an hour

Heat the olive oil over medium heat in a 10-inch non-stick skillet that can later be covered. Add the endives and cook, turning frequently, until they begin to brown. Add the ham and stock, along with some salt and pepper, cover, and cook over the lowest possible heat, turning occasionally, until very tender, about 45 minutes. Uncover, cook out any remaining liquid, drizzle with lemon juice or vinegar, and serve.

Variations

Braised Endive with Anchovies: Sauté 3 or 4 anchovy fillets in the olive oil until they break apart before adding the endive. Omit ham. Add the stock or water and proceed as in original recipe. Finish with lemon juice, or if you like, a drizzling of the Anchovy Caper Vinaigrette from page 99.

Braised Endive with Garlic and Spices or Herbs: Sauté 1 teaspoon minced garlic in the olive oil until it colors lightly before adding the endive. Omit ham. Add a sprinkling of fresh herbs—tarragon, marjoram, parsley, chervil, lovage, or chives—or a pinch of powdered spice such as cumin, curry, or cardomom. Add stock or water and proceed as in original recipe.

⊙ ⊙ ⊙ ⊙ ⊙ ⊙

You can braise almost any green (see the cabbage recipes, page 125, and the alternative greens, below), but there's something so neat about Belgian endive, distinctive in its own little package.

⊙ ⊙ ⊙ ⊙ ⊙ ⊙ ⊙

Sauerkraut Braised in Wine

2 tablespoons lard or lightly
   flavored oil
1½ to 2 pounds sauerkraut,
   rinsed
1 onion, peeled and sliced

1 bay leaf
1 teaspoon juniper berries
1 cup fruity wine, such as
   gewurtraminer or riesling

Makes 4 servings

Time: About 40 minutes

Heat the lard or oil over medium heat until hot, and add the sauerkraut and onion; toss until the onion begins to wilt. Add the remaining ingredients, stir, and cook until some of the wine bubbles away, a minute or 2. Cover, lower the heat, and cook until the sauerkraut is tender, about 30 minutes. Serve immediately.

Variations

Sauerkraut with Bacon and Caraway: Sauté ¼ pound good quality, diced bacon (do not use lard or oil). Remove the bacon with a slotted spoon, set it aside, and add the sauerkraut and onions to the bacon fat; omit the bay leaf and juniper and add 1 tablespoon caraway seeds. Proceed as in original recipe, adding the bacon bits at the end.

Sauerkraut with Bacon and Porcini Mushrooms: Begin as in the first variation. Soak ¼ cup dried porcini mushrooms in 1 cup hot water for a few minutes, until softened; drain, reserving the soaking liquid, trim and chop. Add the mushrooms to the bacon along with the sauerkraut and onion. Use 1 bay leaf and ½ teaspoon dried thyme (or several sprigs fresh thyme) for seasoning. Use the soaking liquid, complemented by a little red wine in place of the white wine. Proceed as in original recipe.

⊙ ⊙ ⊙ ⊙ ⊙ ⊙

You can braise sauerkraut according to any of the recipes for Braised Cabbage (page 125), but sauerkraut takes well to a variety of unusual flavors such as those of juniper berries and fruitier wines.

⊙ ⊙ ⊙ ⊙ ⊙ ⊙ ⊙

Spinach Tossed with Lime and Chiles

2 tablespoons peanut oil
1 1/2 pounds spinach, trimmed, washed, and dried according to the directions on page 39
1 tablespoon crushed red pepper flakes, or to taste

1 teaspoon sugar
Salt and freshly ground black pepper
1 teaspoon minced garlic
1/4 cup lime juice

Makes 4 servings
Time: About 10 minutes

Heat the oil in a large skillet until it begins to smoke. Add the spinach and stir constantly until it wilts, about a minute. Add the red pepper, sugar, salt, pepper, garlic, and lime juice, and cook another 30 seconds or so, still stirring. Serve immediately.

Variation

Spinach with Lime and Cilantro: Before the oil smokes, add 1 onion, peeled and diced; cook until it is soft. Raise the heat to high, brown the onion a bit, and add the spinach as above, with 1 cup minced cilantro. Omit the red pepper, sugar, and garlic; proceed as in original recipe.

Other greens to use:

Chard.

⊙ ⊙ ⊙ ⊙ ⊙ ⊙

A quick, easy preparation taught to me by Chris Schlesinger. You can make this as hot as you like, but don't omit the sugar, a "secret ingredient" that brings all the other flavors together.

⊙ ⊙ ⊙ ⊙ ⊙ ⊙ ⊙

Puréed Cabbage with Cream

1½ pounds green or Savoy
  cabbage, cored and roughly
  chopped
2 tablespoons butter
1 tablespoon minced shallots
1 cup cream

A tiny grating of nutmeg
Salt and freshly ground
  black pepper
1 teaspoon fresh lemon juice

Makes 4 servings
Time: About 30 minutes

Bring a large pot of water to a boil, salt it, and cook the cabbage until it is tender but not waterlogged, about 15 minutes. Drain well. Melt the butter in a large skillet over medium heat and cook the shallots until soft. Add the cabbage and toss to blend.

Purée the cabbage mixture with a little of the cream; return it to the stove, add the remaining cream along with the nutmeg, and reheat gently. Add the salt and pepper to taste, drizzle with the lemon juice, and serve.

One of those old-fashioned dishes that still seems worth doing, this is wonderful with a piece of simply broiled fish.

Grilled Radicchio

2 heads radicchio, about
  ½ pound total
4 to 6 tablespoons olive oil

2 cloves garlic, split in half
Salt and freshly ground
  black pepper

Makes 4 servings
Time: About 20 minutes

Start a charcoal fire or preheat a gas grill or broiler. Trim the radicchio of any damaged leaves and cut it in quarters through the root. Brush each portion liberally with the olive oil and rub with a piece of garlic; sprinkle with salt and pepper. Broil (at least 6 inches from the heat source) or grill, turning frequently, until nicely browned and quite tender, about 12 to 15 minutes total.

One of the few trendy dishes of the '80s that deservedly seems destined to stay with us.

Other greens to use:

Beglian endive or any other heading chicory or endive. You can do this with small heads of cabbage or romaine as well.

Baked Chard in Bechamel

The stalks taken from 2
    pounds of green chard
1 tablespoon butter
1 tablespoon flour
Salt and freshly ground
    black pepper

1 cup whole milk
Dash of freshly grated
    nutmeg
¼ teaspoon cayenne
½ cup bread crumbs,
    preferably fresh

Makes 4 servings
Time: About 40 minutes

Set a pot of water to boil and salt it. Cut the chard into 2-inch pieces and parboil (pages 8-9) until just tender. Drain well and place in a small ovenproof dish. Preheat the oven to 375°F.

Meanwhile, melt the butter in a small saucepan; add the flour and a bit of salt and pepper and cook over medium heat, stirring constantly, for about a minute. Add the milk a little at a time, whisking after each addition until the mixture is smooth. Cook over medium-low heat, stirring, until the mixture thickens slightly. Add the nutmeg and cayenne and pour the mixture over the chard. Top with bread crumbs and bake until the mixture is hot and the bread crumbs lightly browned, about 12 to 15 minutes. Serve immediately.

○ ○ ○ ○ ○ ○ ○

This recipe is unusual in that it uses only the stalks of the chard; save the greens to make the Swiss Chard Pie (page 149) or Chard Frittata with Herbs (page 135) or use them in any spinach dish.

○ ○ ○ ○ ○ ○ ○

Variation

Baked Chard, Provence Style: The southern European version of this dish. Parboil the chard stalks as above, but season the cooking water with a tablespoon of vinegar and a few sprigs of thyme; reserve a cup of the cooking water when the chard is done. Meanwhile, sauté 1 peeled and sliced medium onion, in 2 tablespoons of olive oil until soft. Add a teaspoon of minced garlic and 4 minced anchovy fillets and heat through. Sprinkle with 2 tablespoons of flour and stir in the reserved cooking water; simmer until slightly thickened and pour over the chard as in original recipe. Top with a few slices of ripe tomato, sprinkle with salt, pepper, and a little olive oil, and bake until bubbly.

Light Dishes

Risotto with Arugula and Shrimp

½ to ¾ pound medium to
  large shrimp

3 cups arugula, washed and
  dried according to the
  directions on pages 6-7

4 to 6 cups light fish or
  chicken stock

4 tablespoons olive oil

1 medium onion, minced

1½ cups Arborio or other
  short-grain rice

Salt and pepper

½ cup dry white wine

2 plum tomatoes, seeded and
  roughly chopped

3 tablespoons butter, softened

Makes 4 servings

Time: 45 minutes

Shell the shrimp and simmer the shells in the stock for 10 minutes; while it is cooking, remove tough stems from the arugula and chop it coarsely. Strain the shrimp stock and keep it warm. Cut each shrimp into 2 or 3 pieces.

In a large saucepan or 12-inch skillet (preferably non-stick), sauté the onion in 2 tablespoons of the oil until it softens. Add the rice and stir until it is coated with oil. Add a little salt and pepper, then the white wine. Stir and let it bubble away. Begin to add the stock, a half cup or so at a time, stirring after each addition and every minute or so. When the stock is just about evaporated, add more. The mixture should be neither soupy nor dry.

Meanwhile, sauté the arugula in the remaining oil until it is limp. When the rice is done—it will take 20 to 30 minutes, and should be slightly al dente—add one more ladleful of stock, then the arugula, shrimp, and tomatoes. Continue to cook until the shrimp turns pink and the stock is just about evaporated; stir in the butter and serve immediately.

Other greens to use:

Dandelions, spinach, mustard, turnips, collards, or a combination, large stems removed.

○ ○ ○ ○ ○ ○ ○

Like pasta, the basic technique for risotto can be applied to most combinations of foods. Arugula and shrimp complement each other nicely, but you could follow the same directions for broccoli raab and diced chicken, for example. See the next recipe for another basic risotto.

○ ○ ○ ○ ○ ○ ○

Risotto with Spinach

1 pound spinach, washed and trimmed according to the directions on pages 6-8
4 tablespoons (½ stick) butter
1 small onion, minced
½ cup dry white wine

1½ cups Arborio or other short-grain rice
3 to 5 cups light chicken or vegetable stock, or in a pinch, water
Salt and pepper

Makes 4 servings
Time: 45 minutes

Steam the spinach until it wilts, about 3 to 5 minutes (page 8). Cool quickly under running water, squeeze dry, and chop coarsely. In a large saucepan or 12-inch skillet (preferably non-stick), melt 2 tablespoons of the butter over medium heat and sauté the onion until it softens.

Add the rice and stir until it is coated with oil. Add the spinach and a little salt and pepper; stir until all ingredients are blended, then add the white wine. Raise the heat to medium high, stir and let the wine bubble away.

Begin to add the stock, a half cup or so at a time, stirring after each addition and every minute or so. When the stock is just about evaporated, add more. The mixture should be neither soupy nor dry. Regulate the heat as necessary. When the rice is done—it will take 20 to 30 minutes, and should be slightly al dente—check for seasoning, stir in the remaining butter, and serve immediately.

Variation

Risotto with Radicchio and Parmesan: Follow original recipe, using one small head radicchio (about ¼ to ⅓ of a pound), shredded, but do not precook. Add the radicchio after the rice and proceed as in original recipe. When the risotto is done, stir in 2 tablespoons of softened butter and ½ cup of freshly grated Parmesan.

Other greens to use:

Almost anything; the key is to be aware of the textural differences; spinach, and the leaves of other tender greens, will almost dissolve during cooking. Radicchio, endive, escarole, and so on will stay rather firm.

Chard Frittata

About 1 pound chard, red or
green, washed and trimmed
according to directions on
pages 6-8
1 clove garlic, minced
Dash freshly grated nutmeg

3 tablespoons olive oil
4 extra-large eggs, or 5 large
1/4 cup freshly grated
Parmesan cheese
Salt and freshly ground
pepper to taste

Makes 3 to 4 servings

Time: 40 minutes

Cut the chard stems into 2- or 3-inch lengths, then coarsely
chop the leaves. Steam or parboil the stems (pages 8-9) until they
are almost tender, then add the chopped leaves. Continue to cook
until both stems and leaves are quite tender. Drain, rinse briefly
under cold water and squeeze dry. Chop into small pieces.

In a 10- or 12-inch non-stick skillet, heat 1 tablespoon of the
oil over medium heat; sauté the chard and garlic until the chard
dries out, about 2 or 3 minutes. Add the nutmeg and remove the
chard from the pan.

In a large bowl, beat the eggs lightly with the cheese, then
add the chard, salt, and pepper. In the same skillet, heat the butter
and the remaining oil over medium heat. When the oil is hot, lower
the heat and add the egg mixture. Cook over very low heat until
the frittata is almost set, 10 to 15 minutes. Run the frittata under
the broiler for about 30 to 60 seconds, until it is just set.

Slide the frittata from the pan to a serving plate (using a
spatula if necessary), and serve hot, at room temperature, or cold.

*Unlike omelets, frittati are great
at room temperature; unlike
quiche, they are easy to make
(and can be served without
embarrassment). This one has
the bright, sweet, and slightly
tangy flavor of chard.*

Variation

Chard Frittata with Herbs: Start with two pounds of chard, strip
the leaves from the stems (pages 7-8), and reserve the stems for
another use such as the Baked Chard in Bechamel, page 130.
Proceed as in original recipe; omit the nutmeg, but add 1/2 cup
minced parsley and 1/2 cup minced chervil or basil to the frittata
mixture. Finish as in original recipe.

Other greens to use:

Beet greens and spinach are the most obvious choices, but you
can follow either the original recipe or the variation with kale,
chard, broccoli raab, or almost any other cooking green.

Oysters Baked with Buttered Spinach

5 tablespoons butter

1 cup minced onion

8 to 12 ounces fresh spinach, washed, large stems removed

Salt and freshly ground black pepper

Grated nutmeg

1 cup heavy or light cream or half-and-half

1 teaspoon minced garlic

24 shucked oysters

½ cup fresh toasted bread crumbs

Makes 4 servings

Time: 30 minutes

Preheat the oven to 450°F. Melt 2 tablespoons of the butter in a large skillet over medium heat and sauté the onion until wilted. Chop the spinach roughly and add it to the skillet; turn the heat to high and cook, stirring, until the spinach wilts. Season with salt, pepper, and nutmeg. Lower the heat and add the cream or half-and-half. Cook, stirring, for 2 minutes. Add the garlic and stir in 1 more tablespoon of butter.

Transfer the spinach to a buttered baking dish. Nestle the oysters in the spinach and top with bread crumbs. Dot with the remaining butter. Bake until the oysters cook through, about 15 minutes.

Other greens to use:

Whatever they are, they must be tender and mild flavored, which limits your choices: Look for young dandelions, small beet greens, or mâche.

o o o o o o o

You can make a slightly more challenging but quite impressive version of this dish by pan grilling the oysters instead of baking them: Just heat a nonstick skillet over high heat until it smokes, then toss in the oysters, 6 at a time; turn them after a minute.

o o o o o o o

Steamed Scallops with Spinach, Leeks, and Lemon Vinaigrette

1 leek

Several sprigs fresh tarragon, or 1 teaspoon dried

1 pound spinach, washed and trimmed according to the directions on pages 6-8

12 to 16 large sea scallops, a pound or more

¼ cup fruity extra virgin olive oil

1 or 2 tablespoons fresh lemon juice

Salt and freshly ground black pepper to taste

Makes 4 servings
Time: 30 minutes

Cut the tough green parts from the leek, then cut the leek into quarters. Wash well, fanning out the leaves to remove all the sand. Cut it into 1-inch sections.

Place half the tarragon in the bottom of a steamer with the leeks and the spinach and steam over hot water until the spinach wilts, 3 to 5 minutes. Slice the scallops in half (through their equator, not their axis) and place them on top of the vegetables.

Steam until the scallops are just opaque, 3 to 5 minutes. Whisk the olive oil with some of the lemon juice, add salt and pepper to taste, and see whether or not you want to add more lemon juice. Spike with the remaining tarragon (minced if it is fresh).

Serve the scallops, spinach, and leeks hot or warm, with a bit of the vinaigrette on top.

○ ○ ○ ○ ○ ○
A fast and elegant restaurant-style dish that combines a number of subtle flavors with wonderful results.
○ ○ ○ ○ ○ ○

Other greens to use:

Anything with tender enough stems to be appetizing after the brief steaming: Young dandelions or arugula, cress or mâche, small beet greens or chard.

Spinach Omelet for One

4 ounces spinach, more or
  less, washed according to the
  directions on pages 6-7
Dash of freshly grated
  nutmeg

2 large eggs
Salt and freshly ground black
  pepper
1 tablespoon butter

Makes 1 serving
Time: 15 minutes

Steam the spinach (page 8) until it just wilts, cool briefly, stir
in the nutmeg, and chop coarsely.

In a small bowl, lightly beat the eggs and a pinch of salt and
pepper with a fork until mixed.

Heat the butter in an 8- to 9-inch non-stick pan over medium-high heat. When butter stops foaming and just begins to
color, pour in the eggs. Wait a few seconds until the edges of the
omelet begin to set. Spread the spinach down the middle of the
egg mixture and shake the pan occasionally as the eggs set; use a
wooden spoon or spatula to pull cooked egg at side of pan in toward center and tilt the pan toward that side so that the uncooked
eggs run to edge of pan. Repeat until the omelet is just set but still
moist on top. Cook the omelet a few more seconds to brown the
bottom.

To fold the omelet, jerk the pan sharply toward you a few
times to slide omelet up far side of pan. Jerk the pan again so that
the far edge just folds over onto itself (or use a fork or spatula to
fold the edge over). Grasp the pan as far down the handle as possible with your palm facing up. Rest the far edge of the pan on a
serving plate and gently roll the omelet onto the plate so that it
gets its final fold and lands seam-side down. Use a fork or spatula
to tuck in any edges. Serve immediately.

Other greens to use:

Anything cooked until it is tender. This is an ideal recipe for
using leftover greens; if you want to get rid of the seasoning
from the first cooking, just rinse them in hot water.

○ ○ ○ ○ ○ ○ ○
*When I'm alone, if I find
spinach in the fridge, whether
fresh or leftover, this is the way
I go. Add freshly grated
Parmesan if you like.*
○ ○ ○ ○ ○ ○ ○

Spinach Gnocchi

10 ounces spinach, cleaned, tough stems removed

3 or 4 medium potatoes, about a pound

Salt and freshly ground black pepper to taste

Dash or tiny grating of nutmeg, about $1/16$ teaspoon

1 cup flour, approximately

About 1 cup any light tomato sauce

Freshly grated Parmesan cheese

Makes 4 small servings, suitable for lunch or an appetizer

Time: 60 minutes

Bring a large pot of water to a boil and add salt. When the water boils, cook the spinach until it wilts and the stems become tender, 30 seconds to 2 minutes. Remove it with a strainer or slotted spoon and immediately plunge it in a bowl of ice water; when the spinach has cooled off, squeeze out the excess water and chop very fine.

Wash the potatoes and cook them in the same water until tender but not mushy, 30 to 40 minutes. (The potatoes can be cooked in advance.) Keep the water hot. Mash the potatoes or put them through a food mill; combine them with the spinach, salt, pepper, and nutmeg. Add the flour a bit at a time, kneading with your hands, until the mixture is no longer extremely sticky (the amount of flour you add will depend on the potatoes). Not enough flour will make gnocchi that fall apart; more will make them firm and light; too much will rob them of flavor. Once they stop sticking, add a little more flour and do a test run, then add more flour if necessary.

Form the gnocchi, by hand, into inch-long oval shapes; cook about 6 at a time, lowering them into the water and removing them with a slotted spoon when they rise to the top, 2 or 3 minutes later. Place them in a warm, shallow bowl and keep warm. When all the gnocchi are cooked, top them with tomato sauce and cheese and serve.

Other greens to use:

Chard or beet greens, leaves only.

Pasta with Broccoli Raab

1 pound broccoli raab, bottom
  stems trimmed
Salt
¼ cup olive oil
3 or 4 large cloves of garlic,
  peeled and thinly sliced

1 teaspoon crushed red
  pepper, or to taste
1 pound ziti or other cut pasta

Makes 4 servings
Time: 30 minutes

Bring a large pot of water to a boil; salt it. Put the broccoli raab in the water and cook it until tender but still bright green, about 5 minutes. Remove it from the water and rinse quickly under cold water.

While the water is coming to a boil, heat the olive oil over low heat in a large, deep skillet. Add the garlic and red pepper and cook just until the garlic begins to sizzle. Turn off the heat.

Cook the pasta in the boiling water, stirring frequently. Chop the greens so that no piece is more than an inch long. Turn the heat under the skillet to medium and heat the greens with the garlic and oil mixture. When the pasta is done, reserve about a cup of the cooking liquid and drain. Add the pasta to the skillet with the greens and toss, adding enough of the pasta cooking liquid to keep the dish moist and saucy. Serve immediately.

⊙ ⊙ ⊙ ⊙ ⊙ ⊙

This simple pasta dish needs no cheese; it is also delicious with turnip or mustard greens.

⊙ ⊙ ⊙ ⊙ ⊙ ⊙ ⊙

Other greens to use:

Mustard, turnip, dandelion, kale, collards.

Pasta with Spinach and Butter

Salt and freshly ground black
  pepper
10 to 16 ounces fresh spinach,
  washed and trimmed
  according to the directions
  on page 39

4 tablespoons ($\frac{1}{2}$ stick) butter
1 pound spaghetti, linguine,
  or fettucine
1 cup heavy cream
1 cup freshly grated
  Parmesan

Makes 4 servings

Time: 30 minutes

Bring a large pot of water to a boil and salt it. Chop the spinach coarsely. Melt 2 tablespoons of the butter over medium heat in a 12-inch skillet that can later be covered and add the spinach. Cover, lower the heat, and cook, stirring occasionally, until nice and soft, about 10 minutes. Uncover, add the cream and cook gently for about 5 minutes.

Meanwhile, cook the pasta until tender but still firm. When it is just about done, put the remaining butter in a large, warmed bowl and add a couple of tablespoons of the cooking water. Drain the pasta and toss it with the butter and half the Parmesan. Add the spinach sauce and serve, passing the remaining Parmesan at the table.

Other greens to use:

None.

○ ○ ○ ○ ○ ○

While the above pasta dish is "strong," this one is creamy and mild.

○ ○ ○ ○ ○ ○ ○

Greens and Beans

½ pound dried white beans
1 onion
1 bay leaf
1 clove
1½ pounds washed greens, roughly chopped

Salt and freshly ground pepper to taste
1 tablespoon minced garlic
4 teaspoons extra virgin olive oil

Makes 4 servings
Time: 2 hours, plus soaking time for the beans

Soak the beans in water to cover for 8 hours or overnight (alternatively, cover them with water, boil for 2 minutes, then soak for two hours). Drain and place in a large pot with water to cover; bring to a boil. Meanwhile, cut a slit in the onion and insert the bay leaf; insert the clove into the onion as well and put the onion in the pot. Simmer, stirring occasionally, until the beans are quite tender, at least an hour; add additional water if necessary.

Add the greens to the pot and continue to cook until they are tender, 10 to 20 minutes, depending on the thickness of the stems. If you want a soupy mixture, add more water. Season to taste with salt and pepper. About 3 minutes before serving, add the garlic and stir. Spoon the beans and greens into individual bowls and drizzle with olive oil. Serve immediately.

○ ○ ○ ○ ○ ○
This is a near-staple in my house.
○ ○ ○ ○ ○ ○ ○

Other greens to use:

This is best with strong-flavored greens such as turnips or mustard, but it's fine with collards, kale, or a mixture of several greens.

Broccoli Raab with Sausage and Grapes

About 1½ pounds broccoli raab, washed and trimmed according to the directions on pages 6-8
About 1 pound fresh, sweet, garlicky sausage

2 cloves garlic, peeled and slivered
About ½ pound seedless grapes
Salt and freshly ground black pepper

Makes 8 appetizer-size servings
Time: About 30 minutes

Parboil (pages 8-9) the broccoli raab for about 3 minutes, until it is bright green and beginning to become tender. Drain and run it under cold water for a few moments.

Meanwhile, heat a 12-inch non-stick skillet over medium-high heat for 3 to 4 minutes; put the sausage in the pan, prick it with a fork or thin-bladed knife a few times, and cook it, turning from time to time, until it is nicely browned.

Remove the sausage from the skillet (don't worry about it being done) and cut it into bite-sized pieces. Return it to the skillet, over medium heat; cook, turning occasionally, until all sides of the sausage are nicely browned, about 5 more minutes.

Squeeze the excess liquid from the broccoli raab and chop it coarsely. Add it to the skillet along with the garlic and cook, stirring occasionally, for 3 or 4 minutes. Add the grapes and heat through. Sprinkle liberally with black pepper and check for salt. Serve immediately.

Other greens to use:

They should be strong-flavored, and the dish is best if they have stems with some chew, also: Mustard, kale, collards, turnips.

◦ ◦ ◦ ◦ ◦ ◦

Sweet, sour, bitter, garlicky— this is a dish that has it all. Use red grapes if you can find them for extra eye appeal.

◦ ◦ ◦ ◦ ◦ ◦

Chard Fritters

1 pound red or green chard, washed and trimmed according to the directions on pages 6-8

Salt and freshly ground black pepper

1 teaspoon minced garlic

½ cup freshly grated Parmesan cheese

Tiny grating of nutmeg

Flour as needed

Oil (preferably olive, but vegetable will do) as needed

Minced parsley for garnish

Lemon wedges

Makes 15 to 20, enough for finger food for 8 to 10

Time: About 40 minutes

Set a large pot of water to boil; salt it well. Separate the greens and stems of the chard (pages 7-8). Cut the stems into 1- or 2-inch lengths; chop the greens coarsely. Parboil the stems until almost tender, about 5 minutes, then add the greens; cook until all are nice and soft, another 3 to 5 minutes. Remove, drain, rinse under cold water, and squeeze thoroughly until dry.

Purée the chard with the garlic in a blender and purée until smooth. Place in a bowl and stir in the Parmesan, nutmeg, salt and pepper to taste (remember that Parmesan is salty), and enough flour to make a stiff mixture that can be shaped into balls.

Add at least an inch of oil to a deep, steep-sided skillet or a pot or a deep fryer; heat to 350°F. Shape the chard mixture into balls and fry until crisp and brown on all sides, a couple of minutes per side. Sprinkle with minced parsley and serve with lemon wedges.

Other greens to use:

Spinach, beet greens.

○ ○ ○ ○ ○ ○ ○

If you've an aversion to fried food, I'm sorry; these are really great. They are even good at room temperature, which is how they often are served in Italy.

○ ○ ○ ○ ○ ○ ○

Pasta with Chickpeas and Kale

1 pound kale, washed and
  trimmed according to the
  directions on pages 6-8
1 tablespoon olive oil
1 tablespoon minced garlic
1 dried hot pepper, optional

4 tablespoons minced parsley
Salt and pepper to taste
1 pound ziti, elbow macaroni,
  twists, or bowties
2 cups cooked chickpeas,
  drained

Makes 4 servings
Time: 40 minutes with
previously cooked chickpeas

Set a large pot of water to boil and salt it. Cut the kale stems
into 2- to 3-inch pieces; chop the leaves coarsely and set aside. Boil
the stems until they are nearly tender, then add the greens. Cook
the kale until it is still bright green but quite tender. Scoop it out
with a slotted spoon and keep the water boiling. When the kale
cools, squeeze out the excess water, gather it into a mass, and chop
it rather finely.

Meanwhile, place the olive oil in a large skillet over very
low heat and add the garlic and optional hot pepper. Cook slowly
until the garlic becomes golden brown, then add 2 tablespoons of
parsley, salt, and pepper. Remove the hot pepper.

While the garlic is cooking, cook the pasta, tasting frequently
to make sure it does not overcook. When it is done, drain it. Warm
the garlic mixture over medium heat and add the pasta, the
chickpeas, and the chopped kale. Toss well, taste for seasoning,
garnish with parsley, and serve immediately.

Other greens to use:

Collards, broccoli raab, turnip, mustard.

Baked Penne with Radicchio and Gorgonzola

1 pound penne or other large
  pasta
2 small heads radicchio, about
  ½ pound, shredded
4 scallions, trimmed and
  slivered
2 cups light cream
1 cup gorgonzola cheese,
  crumbled

1 cup freshly grated
  Parmesan
Salt and freshly grated
  black pepper
Butter
½ cup bread crumbs,
  preferably fresh

Makes 4 servings
Time: About an hour

Bring a large pot of water to a boil, salt it liberally, and cook
the pasta until it is tender but still has some bite. Drain it well;
preheat the oven to 375°F. Mix the pasta with the radicchio, scallions, cream, gorgonzola, and half the Parmesan. Taste for salt (it
may not need any) and add pepper to taste.

Grease a baking pan with butter and pour in the pasta mixture. Mix together the bread crumbs and remaining Parmesan and
spread this on top of the pasta. Bake for about 30 minutes, until
the mixture is hot, then raise the heat to 450°F and continue to
bake until the bread crumb mixture browns nicely, another 10
minutes or so. Serve immediately.

Other greens to use:

This is a recipe for tough "salad" greens: Endive, escarole, or
chicory.

Pancotto ("Cooked Bread")

4 cups leftover cooked greens
(it's okay if they were
seasoned with garlic, oil,
herbs, and salt; if they were
seasoned otherwise, pour
hot water over them to
rinse)

3 cups leftover bread, roughly
chopped into crumbs
1/3 cup olive oil
1 tablespoon minced garlic
Salt and freshly ground
black pepper

Makes 4 servings
Time: About 35 minutes

Preheat the oven to 400°F. Toss the greens in an ovenproof
dish with 2 cups of the bread crumbs, the olive oil, and the garlic;
season to taste. Chop or grind the rest of the bread crumbs and use
them to top the dish. Bake until nice and brown, about 20 to 30
minutes; run under the broiler to brown further if you like.

Variation

Cooked Bread with Potatoes and Red Pepper: Add a couple of
cups of boiled peeled potatoes to the mixture, and increase the
olive oil accordingly. You can cook this on top of the stove in a
skillet if you like, as if it were a hash (which, in fact, it is). Season
liberally with red pepper flakes.

⊚ ⊚ ⊚ ⊚ ⊚ ⊚

*A mixture of leftovers my
mother might call
"gummage"—a word I'm
pretty sure she made up—and
my friend Tim would call,
somewhat less flatteringly,
"grout." Forget mashed
potatoes; this defines comfort
food.*

⊚ ⊚ ⊚ ⊚ ⊚ ⊚

Pizzocheri with Savoy Cabbage, Potatoes, and Taleggio

Salt and freshly ground black
  pepper
1 pound Savoy cabbage, cored
  and shredded
2 potatoes, peeled and diced
3 tablespoons butter

5 sage leaves, preferably fresh
1 pound pizzocheri or other
  pasta
1 cup grated taleggio
1 cup grated Parmesan

Makes 4 servings
Time: 30 to 40 minutes

Bring a large pot of water to the boil and salt it. Add the potatoes and the cabbage. When they are tender, about 10 minutes later, remove them with a slotted spoon and place them in a large bowl; season with pepper and a little salt and keep warm.

Put the butter and sage in a small saucepan and simmer while you cook the pasta. Cook the pasta until tender but still firm. Just before the pasta is done, remove a half cup of the cooking liquid and pour over the cabbage and potatoes. Drain the pasta and add it to the vegetables, along with the taleggio and half the Parmesan. Pour the butter-sage mixture over all, top with grated pepper, and serve, tossing at the table and passing the remaining Parmesan.

Other greens to use:

Green, red, or any Chinese cabbage; adjust the initial cooking time accordingly.

o o o o o o o

If you can't find pizzocheri, a buckwheat pasta cut like fettucine, substitute any large pasta. If you can't find taleggio (already a compromise, because when I had this dish it was made with a local Alpine cheese whose name only exists in dialect), use real fontina.

o o o o o o o

Swiss Chard Pie

2 pounds of green or red
  chard greens (for stems, see
  recipes on pages 135, 144)
2 cups flour
Salt and freshly ground
  black pepper
½ cup olive oil, plus a
  little more

Cold water as needed
2 eggs
1 small onion, peeled and
  minced
¼ cup minced fresh basil,
  if available
½ cup freshly grated
  Parmesan cheese

Makes 4 servings
Time: About an hour

Preheat the oven to 350°F. Parboil (pages 8-9) the chard; drain, run it under cold water to chill, squeeze it dry, and chop it coarsely.

Mix the flour and a teaspoon of salt in a mixing bowl; using a fork, stir in the olive oil until well blended. Add the water a little at a time until you can gather the dough into a ball. Cut the dough in half. Use a little olive oil to grease the bottom of an 8- or 9-inch pie pan. Roll out half the dough and lay it into the pan, with the edges hanging over a bit.

Mix together the chard, eggs, cheese, salt, pepper, onion, and basil and pour the mixture into the pie crust. Spread it out. Roll out the other half of the dough and top the pie with it; crimp the edges together and trim any excess dough. Cut the top crust with a scissors and bake until nicely browned, 25 to 40 minutes. Serve hot or at room temperature.

Other greens to use:

Spinach, dandelion, cress, as long as the stems are very tender.

◎ ◎ ◎ ◎ ◎ ◎ ◎

You can use any pie crust you like for this traditional Provencal dish, but I like this one, which is based on olive oil. It's best made by hand; using a food processor will really toughen the dough.

◎ ◎ ◎ ◎ ◎ ◎ ◎

Spinach Pasta

5 ounces fresh spinach,
washed and trimmed
according to the directions
on page 39

2 cups all-purpose flour
1 teaspoon salt
3 large eggs, beaten

Makes about a pound
Time: 30 minutes including cutting

Steam the spinach (page 8), run it under cold water until it is cool enough to handle, and squeeze until completely dry; chop finely.

Pulse the flour and salt in the workbowl of a food processor; add the eggs and spinach and process until a ball forms, about 30 seconds; add a few drops of water if necessary.

Turn the dough out onto a dry, lightly floured work surface and knead until it is smooth, just a minute or two. Cut a quarter of the dough off and wrap the rest in plastic wrap. Flatten the dough and roll it out with a pin until almost sheer or run it through a pasta machine, repeatedly narrowing the distance between the rollers, until the dough is very thin and almost translucent. Use flour as necessary, but not more than you must. Repeat with the remaining dough.

Cut the pasta into any shape you desire and cook immediately or dry for a few hours before cooking or storing.

Other greens to use:

Red chard or beet greens, greens only (your pasta will be pinkish red, which is nice); green chard, greens only.

Stuffed Grape Leaves

40 to 50 nice large
  grape leaves
2 tablespoons fruity olive oil,
  plus more for garnish
1 medium onion, peeled and
  diced
¼ cup pine nuts
1 cup rice
½ teaspoon allspice

Salt and freshly ground
  black pepper
1½ cups stock (preferred) or
  water
2 tablespoons minced fresh
  mint or dill (or 1 teaspoon
  dried)
¼ cup lemon juice

Makes about 30, enough for 10 to 15 people
as an appetizer
Time: At least an hour and a half; this is a project

Parboil the grape leaves, a few at a time, until they are tender and pliable. Cut off the stems, and remove any hard veins near the base of the leaves. Pat dry with paper towels.

Meanwhile, heat the olive oil in a pot and sauté the onion until it is tender. Add the pine nuts, rice, allspice, and a teaspoon of salt, the water or stock, cover, and cook until the rice is somewhat tender but still quite al dente, about 10 to 12 minutes. Cool in a large bowl, check for salt, and add lots of pepper, the mint or dill, and half the lemon juice.

One at a time, place the grape leaves, shiny side down, and put a dab—not too big, just a tablespoon or so—of the rice mixture in the middle of the leaf. Fold over the stem end, then the sides, then roll toward the tip, making a neat little package. Don't roll too tightly, as the rice will continue to expand during subsequent cooking.

Place the packages side by side in a roasting pan or skillet (you can layer them if you like), add water (or even better, more stock) to come about halfway up the rolls, and weight with a plate. Cover the pan or skillet and cook over low heat for 30 minutes or so, until most of the liquid is absorbed.

Serve at room temperature, sprinkled with remaining lemon juice and a bit of olive oil.

Other greens to use:

As noted above, cabbage (any kind with big leaves and thin stems), chard, or thin-stemmed collards or kale.

◦ ◦ ◦ ◦ ◦ ◦ ◦

I don't like grape leaves from a jar; you still need to parboil them, and they have no flavor whatsoever. Unless you can get fresh grape leaves (which are not that hard to find in most parts of the country), make this with cabbage or chard. You can use this technique to stuff grape leaves with almost anything (see the suggestions for stuffed cabbage, page 180), but well-seasoned rice with pine nuts is the standard.

◦ ◦ ◦ ◦ ◦ ◦ ◦

Main Courses

Stir-fried Chicken with Peanuts and Hiziki

¾ pound boneless chicken
  breast
½ cup hiziki, rinsed and
  soaked in warm water until
  soft, about 5 minutes
2 tablespoons peanut oil
2 cloves garlic, minced

3 dried red peppers, or to
  taste
½ cup peanuts
½ cup chicken or vegetable
  stock, or water
2 tablespoons high-quality
  soy sauce (tamari)

Makes 4 servings

Time: About 20 minutes

Cube the meat into bite-sized pieces; roughly chop the hiziki. In a wok or large skillet, heat the oil over high heat just until it begins to smoke. Add the garlic and peppers; stir.

Add the chicken and cook, stirring, until the chicken loses its color. Add the hiziki and peanuts and stir. Add the stock or water and let it bubble away for a minute or so. Add the tamari, correct the seasoning, and serve immediately over rice.

I like to make this dish when there are no fresh vegetables in the house; it takes advantage of the convenience and intense flavor of dried hiziki.

Other greens to use:

Arame.

Braised Bok Choi

1 tablespoon peanut oil

2 cloves garlic, smashed or minced

4 nickel-sized slices ginger

2 bok choi, washed and trimmed according to the directions on pages 6-8

1 tablespoon hoisin sauce (available at Asian markets)

1 tablespoon soy sauce

1 teaspoon sugar

1 teaspoon rice or wine vinegar

1/2 cup water

3 scallions, trimmed and cut into 1-inch lengths

Makes 4 servings

Time: About 20 minutes

Cut the stems of the bok choi into one-inch sections; coarsely chop the leaves and set them aside.

Heat a wok or large skillet over medium-high heat until it begins to smoke. Add the oil, garlic, and ginger, and stir for 10 seconds. Add the bok choi stems and cook, stirring, until they begin to brown, 2 or 3 minutes. Lower the heat to medium, add the hoisin sauce, soy sauce, sugar, vinegar, and water, and then stir to blend. Cover and cook over medium-low heat until the stems are tender, about 10 minutes.

Uncover, raise heat to high, add the leaves, and cook, stirring, until the sauce has all but evaporated. Toss in the scallions, cook another minute or so, and serve.

○ ○ ○ ○ ○ ○

This braised dish brings out all the creaminess of thick-stemmed Chinese cabbage. Serve it with rice as a vegetarian main course, with a stir-fry, or with grilled or broiled fish.

○ ○ ○ ○ ○ ○

Other greens to use:

You can braise almost any green, of course, but few greens have the magnificent texture of bok-choi stems. Chard is the closest, but the taste is quite different.

Roast Chicken Breast with Sautéed and Roasted Savoy Cabbage

1 small head green or Savoy cabbage, about 2 pounds

2 tablespoons plus 1 teaspoon olive oil or peanut oil

1 teaspoon minced ginger

1 teaspoon minced garlic

Salt and freshly ground black pepper

One large boneless chicken breast, a pound or more, trimmed of fat

1 tablespoon roasted sesame oil

Chopped scallion for garnish

Makes 4 servings

Time: 40 minutes

Preheat the oven to 450°F. Shred the cabbage, then chop it coarsely. Divide it in half, and chop one half a little more finely. In a 12-inch skillet sauté the coarsely chopped cabbage in the 2 tablespoons of oil over medium-high heat until softened. Add the ginger and garlic and continue to cook until the cabbage is slightly browned. Add salt and pepper; cover and keep warm.

While the cabbage is cooking, use the remaining olive oil or peanut oil to lightly grease the bottom of a baking dish slightly larger than the chicken. Cover the bottom of the dish with the finely chopped cabbage. Sprinkle with salt, then lay the chicken on top; salt the chicken lightly. Roast for 12 to 15 minutes until the chicken is almost done; it will be firm to the touch but not rubbery. Scatter the sautéed cabbage around the chicken and roast another 2 minutes. Sprinkle with sesame oil and chopped scallions; serve immediately.

⊙ ⊙ ⊙ ⊙ ⊙ ⊙ ⊙

In this inexpensive but elegant dish the cabbage, half of which is sautéed and half roasted, lends a lovely sweetness to the chicken.

⊙ ⊙ ⊙ ⊙ ⊙ ⊙ ⊙

Other greens to use:

Any head cabbage, or Napa cabbage.

Cornish Hens on a Bed of Savoy Cabbage

¼-pound slab bacon, in
  one piece
2 onions, peeled and diced
2 cornish hens
1 pound Savoy or red cab-
  bage, cored and shredded
1 cup dry white wine

Several juniper berries
2 bay leaves
Several peppercorns
Several sprigs of fresh thyme,
  or 1 teaspoon dried
Salt and freshly ground
  black pepper

Makes 4 servings
Time: About an hour and a quarter

Cut the bacon into ½-inch dice; in a large skillet, sauté it over medium heat until it is crisp all over, then add the onions. Continue to cook, stirring, until the onion softens. Using a slotted spoon, remove the onions and bacon to a Dutch oven or an oven-proof casserole.

Preheat the oven to 350°F. Dry the cornish hens and brown them all over in the bacon fat; place them in the casserole on top of the onions. Sauté the cabbage quickly in the remaining bacon fat, just until it begins to wilt. Scatter it around the hens.

Add the wine to the pan and cook over high heat, stirring with a wooden spoon, until the wine is reduced by half. Moisten the cabbage with this. Tie the juniper berries, bay leaves, pepper-corns, and thyme in a cheesecloth and tuck it into the cabbage. Sprinkle the whole dish with salt and pepper.

Cover and bake until the hens are nearly done, about 40 minutes; remove the top from the casserole, raise the heat to 400°F; and let the birds brown a little on top. Remove the cheesecloth bag and serve immediately.

Variations

Rabbit with Red Cabbage: Substitute 1 rabbit, cut up, for the hens. Use red cabbage and red wine. Reduce baking time by 50 percent; finish with a tablespoon of top-quality wine vinegar.

Duck with Savoy Cabbage: Use a whole duck, washed, dried, and with as much surface fat removed as possible. Use Savoy or red cabbage and a fruity, not-quite-dry wine such as Riesling. Increase baking time by about 50 percent.

Fried Chicken with Peanuts and Nori

Oil for shallow frying

2 sheets nori seaweed
(available in Asian markets
and health food stores)

1/2 cup roasted peanuts

Salt if needed

1 pound boneless chicken
breast 1/2-inch chunks

Flour for dredging

2 eggs, lightly beaten

Lemon wedges

Makes 2 to 4 servings

Time: 30 minutes

Add enough oil to a 10- or 12-inch skillet to reach a depth of at least 1/2 inch; heat it over medium-high heat to between 350°F and 370°F.

As the oil is heating, toast the nori by running it a couple of inches above an open flame several times. It will become brittle. Break it into large pieces, and in a food processor, crumble it with the peanuts; do not purée. Salt the mixture if the peanuts were unsalted.

Dry the chicken pieces thoroughly. Dredge them in flour, then dip them in egg, then roll them in the peanut-nori mixture. Plan to cook the chicken in a couple of batches, unless you are using a large skillet; fry, turning as each side browns, for a total of 5 or 6 minutes. Drain on paper towels and serve immediately with lots of lemon, or keep warm while you cook the remainder.

o o o o o o o

A crunchy and flavorful dish; if you've only had nori as a sushi wrapper, you're in for a pleasant surprise.

o o o o o o o

Fish Fillets en Papillote with Spinach

About 1 pound spinach, washed and trimmed according to the directions on page 39

6 fillets of white fish, 4 to 6 ounces each

6 sun-dried tomatoes, reconstituted in warm water for 15 minutes

Salt and freshly ground black pepper

12 fresh tarragon leaves, or about 1/2 teaspoon dried tarragon

6 teaspoons olive oil, approximately

Makes 6 servings

Time: 60 minutes

Steam the spinach in the water clinging to its leaves, just until it wilts. (Don't worry about cooking it; the idea is to shrink it so that it fits in the package.) Preheat the oven to 450°F. Tear off a 1-foot square piece of aluminum foil (the more traditional parchment paper is, of course, acceptable). Place a portion of spinach, roughly the same size as the fillet, on the foil; top with a piece of fish, a tomato, salt and pepper, tarragon, and a drizzle of oil. Seal the package and repeat the process.

Place all the packages in a large baking dish and bake for about 30 minutes, until the fish is white, opaque, and tender. Serve closed packages, allowing diners to open their own at the table.

Other greens to use:

Arugula, chard (leaves only), dandelion.

○ ○ ○ ○ ○ ○

There are few cooking methods as fun as this one, which has the added advantage of being virtually foolproof. Since seasonings can be minimal, the flavor of the fish and the greens come to the fore. And you can use almost any white fillet you can find here, from flounder to rockfish to perch to red snapper.

○ ○ ○ ○ ○ ○

Grilled Wasabe Swordfish with Spinach and Soy

1½ teaspoons wasabe powder
  (available in Asian markets)
1 tablespoon water
1 tablespoon sesame seeds
1 pound cleaned spinach
2 tablespoons natural
  soy sauce

4 6-ounce swordfish steaks,
  or 1 or 2 larger ones, cut up
  to make 4 steaks
Juice of ½ lemon
Salt and freshly ground
  black pepper
2 scallions, finely minced

Makes 4 servings
Time: 45 minutes

Build a hot charcoal or wood fire, or preheat a gas grill until it is as hot as you can make it. Set a large pot of water to boil. Mix together the wasabe and the tablespoon of water and set aside for a few minutes. Toast the sesame seeds: Heat them, dry, in a small skillet over medium heat, shaking occasionally, until they darken and begin to pop, about 5 minutes.

When the water boils, plunge the spinach into it and cook just for a minute or two. Remove it and place in a bowl of ice water. Drain, chop, and mix with 1 tablespoon of the soy sauce and half the sesame seeds; spread on a platter.

Using a knife or small spatula, spread the wasabe on the swordfish. Sprinkle with a little salt and pepper and grill about 4 minutes per side. Check for doneness by peeking between the layers of flesh with a thin-bladed knife—when the knife meets little resistance and no translucence remains, the swordfish is done.

Lay the cooked fish atop the spinach. Drizzle with the remaining soy sauce and the lemon juice. Garnish with the remaining sesame seeds and the minced scallion, and serve.

Other greens to use:

Chard is the best substitute here, but you can use arugula, cress, dandelion, any lettuce, or a mesclun mixture, without cooking—the heat of the grilled fish will wilt the greens a little, which is fine.

○ ○ ○ ○ ○ ○

Wasabe, the dried horseradish used in sushi, is extremely hot; be very careful when handling it. Keep the powder in a closed container, where it will remain potent practically forever.

○ ○ ○ ○ ○ ○

Grilled Mesclun-stuffed Tuna Steaks

Juice of 2 limes

1/4 cup soy sauce

1 medium clove garlic, minced

1 teaspoon strong mustard

2 teaspoons ginger, finely minced, or 1 teaspoon dried

1/2 teaspoon sesame oil

1/2 teaspoon black pepper, coarsely ground

1/4 cup dry white wine or water

1 tuna steak, no less than 1 1/4 inches thick, about 1 1/2 pounds

About 1 1/2 cups assorted greens, washed and dried according to the directions on pages 6-7

Makes 4 servings

Time: 20 minutes

Start a charcoal or wood fire or preheat a gas grill or broiler. Mix together all the ingredients except the tuna and the greens.

Using a sharp, thin-bladed knife (a boning knife, for example), make a small incision halfway down any edge of the tuna steak. Insert the knife almost to the opposite edge of the steak, then move it back and forth, flipping it over and creating a large pocket. Be careful not to cut through the top, bottom, or opposite edge of the tuna. Put the tuna in the soy mixture; you can leave it there for a few minutes or continue with the recipe right away.

Remove the tuna from the liquid and dry it with paper towels. Toss the mesclun with the marinade. Stuff the pocket with the mesclun, still drenched in the liquid. Seal the pocket opening with a couple of toothpicks. Grill the tuna, turning once, about 5 minutes per inch of thickness (if your steak is 1 1/2 inches thick, for example, turn it after about 4 minutes and cook 3 or 4 minutes more). It will be quite rare; if you want to cook it more, go right ahead. Serve, cut into quarters or 1/2-inch thick slices.

⊙ ⊙ ⊙ ⊙ ⊙ ⊙

This is a gorgeous dish that is incredibly fast to make and pleases everyone (if you can't find tuna or have some fish-haters around, use tenderloin of beef). Do not be intimidated by the creation of the pocket; it is easy, and takes just a minute.

⊙ ⊙ ⊙ ⊙ ⊙ ⊙ ⊙

Other greens to use:

Arugula, cress, dandelion, or any lettuces.

Red-Cooked Collards

1 cup dark soy sauce or
  tamari
1 cup water
½ cup dry sherry
Several nickel-sized pieces of
  fresh ginger

4 or 5 cloves garlic
1 tablespoon sugar
Several pieces of star anise
2 pounds collard greens

Makes 4 main-course servings or
8 smaller servings
Time: 30 minutes

Combine first 7 ingredients in a large pot and bring to a boil. Continue to boil while you prepare the collards. After washing the greens, trim them of their large stems (pages 7-8) and chop coarsely. Place in the cooking liquid and adjust heat to maintain a gentle boil. Cook until the greens are tender and most of the liquid is gone, about 10 to 15 minutes. Serve over rice as a main coarse or as a side dish.

○ ○ ○ ○ ○ ○ ○

A traditional Chinese cooking technique that is usually used for meats but is excellent with the tougher greens.

○ ○ ○ ○ ○ ○ ○

Other greens to use:

Broccoli raab, any of the thick-stemmed cabbages, or kale.

Beef Braised with Kale, Cepes, and Soy

An ounce of dried porcini (cepes), or about ¼ pound fresh wild mushrooms

½ pound kale, washed and trimmed according to the directions on pages 6-8

1 tablespoon olive or peanut oil

½ pound thinly sliced sirloin or tenderlion

2 tablespoons natural soy sauce

1 tablespoon vinegar

2 tablespoons water

Salt and freshly ground black pepper

Makes 4 servings

Time: About 20 minutes

Reconstitute the dried mushrooms in hot water to cover for about 10 minutes; drain, reserving the soaking liquid. Trim any hard parts and chop. Chop the kale into bite-sized pieces, discarding any stems that are thicker than an eighth of an inch or so.

Heat the oil over medium heat in a 10- or 12-inch non-stick skillet that can later be covered. When it shimmers, toss in the meat and the mushrooms. Stir just until the meat begins to lose its redness, about a minute. Add the kale, ¼ cup of the reserved mushroom liquid (or water or stock if you used fresh mushrooms), soy sauce, vinegar, and water, and stir. Bring to a boil, lower the heat, cover, and simmer for about 5 minutes. Check and adjust the seasoning and serve.

Other greens to use:

Bok choi or chard.

○ ○ ○ ○ ○ ○ ○

A quick East-West style dish that is best served with rice.

○ ○ ○ ○ ○ ○ ○

Stir-fried Shrimp with Bok Choi and Black Beans

1 pound large shrimp,
  shell on
1½ teaspoons sugar
2 tablespoons soy sauce
1 clove garlic, sliced
1 teaspoon salt
2 teaspoons sesame oil
1 pound bok choi, washed
  and trimmed according to
  the directions on pages 6-7

2 tablespoons minced garlic
2 tablespoons peanut oil
1 tablespoon peeled and
  minced ginger
1 tablespoon fermented
  black beans, soaked in 2
  tablespoons dry sherry
¼ cup minced scallions

Makes 4 servings

Time: 30 minutes

Peel the shrimp and simmer the peels for 5 minutes or so in a cup of water. Marinate the shrimp in ½ teaspoon of the sugar, 1 tablespoon of the soy sauce, the sliced garlic, salt, and a teaspoon of the sesame oil while you assemble the other ingredients. Drain the shrimp peels, reserving ¾ cup of the stock.

Separate the bok choi leaves from the stems (pages 7-8), and parboil (pages 8-9) the stems for a couple of minutes; rinse them in cold water and drain.

Preheat a wok or 12-inch non-stick skillet over medium-high heat for 3 to 5 minutes. Add a tablespoon of peanut oil and raise heat to high. When it begins to smoke, add the minced garlic, the shrimp, and its marinade. Cook the shrimp about 1 minute per side, over high heat. Spoon it out of the wok or skillet.

Put the remaining oil in the wok or skillet, and when it smokes, add the ginger and bok choi stems. Cook, stirring, until the bok choi is lightly browned, 3 to 5 minutes, then add the greens. Cook, stirring, for a minute, then add the shrimp stock and let it bubble away for a minute or 2. Return the shrimp to the wok and stir; add the black beans, the scallions, and the remaining sugar and soy sauce. Stir and cook for a minute. Turn off the heat, drizzle over the remaining sesame oil, and serve.

Other greens to use:

Broccoli raab or chard; you could also use collards or kale if you parboil the stems a little longer.

⊙ ⊙ ⊙ ⊙ ⊙ ⊙

This is one instance where you should be certain to buy shell-on shrimp so you can use the shells to make a quick stock, which greatly enhances this dish's flavor.

⊙ ⊙ ⊙ ⊙ ⊙ ⊙

Lasagna with Endive and Radicchio

1½ cups milk

3 tablespoons unsalted butter

2¾ cups flour

Salt

1 tablespoon olive oil

1 onion, chopped fine

2 cloves garlic, minced

⅓ pound pancetta or bacon, cut into ½-inch squares

1½ pounds Belgian endive, roots trimmed and leaves cut into ¼-inch-wide strips

About 1 pound radicchio, cored and cut into ¼-inch wide strips

½ teaspoon freshly ground black pepper

Salt to taste

18 dried lasagna noodles

¾ pound Gruyere cheese, shredded

Makes 6 to 8 servings
Time: About an hour and a quarter

Make the bechamel: Warm the milk in a small pan or microwave; meanwhile, heat the butter in a medium-sized saucepan. When it is foamy, whisk in the flour until smooth. Stir and cook for 2 minutes over medium heat. Do not let the flour brown.

Add several tablespoons of the hot milk, whisking constantly. When the milk is thoroughly blended into the butter and flour mixture, add several more tablespoons. Repeat until all the milk has been added and the sauce is smooth. If at any time the sauce separates or lumps form, whisk vigorously until smooth.

Add the salt and cook the sauce over medium heat for several minutes or until it thickens slightly and has the texture of heavy cream. Do not let it bubble. Remove the pan from the heat.

Heat the olive oil in a large saucepan. Add the onion and sauté over medium heat until translucent, about 5 minutes. Stir in the garlic and pancetta and continue cooking over medium heat for about 3 minutes, stirring occasionally so pancetta squares separate.

Stir in the endive and coat well with oil. Sauté, stirring occasionally so cooked endive is pulled to the top of the pan, until all the endive is wilted, about 7 minutes. Add radicchio and stir constantly until radicchio loses its bright red color and softens, about 2 minutes. Stir in pepper and taste for salt. Set the mixture aside.

○ ○ ○ ○ ○ ○ ○

A lovely recipe adapted from my good friend Jack Bishop, an Italian cook who combines intuition and tradition brilliantly.

○ ○ ○ ○ ○ ○ ○

Cook and drain the pasta; preheat the oven to 400°F. Grease a 9-inch by 13-inch lasagna pan. Smear 3 tablespoons of the bechamel across the bottom. Cover with a layer of pasta, making sure noodles touch but do not overlap. Spread 1 cup endive and radicchio mixture over noodles. Drizzle with 3 tablespoons bechamel and sprinkle with ½ cup cheese. Repeat layering of the pasta, vegetables, bechamel, and cheese 4 more times. For the sixth layer, coat pasta with 6 tablespoons bechamel and sprinkle with remaining cup cheese.

Bake the lasagna until the cheese turns golden brown in spots, 20 to 25 minutes. Remove the pan from the oven, let the lasagna settle for 5 minutes, and serve.

Other greens to use:

Escarole, frisee, or anything from the chicory-endive family.

Capon and Cabbage

1 capon or large roasting chicken, 6 to 10 pounds

A few sprigs of fresh thyme, or 1 teaspoon dried

1 bay leaf

Salt to taste

1 teaspoon whole black peppercorns

2 cloves

2 large white onions

2 stalks of celery

2 cups dry white wine

1 2-pound head of cabbage, outer leaves removed, quartered

1 large leek, thoroughly cleaned and coarsely chopped

2 carrots, trimmed and scraped

6 small potatoes, whole, scrubbed, jackets left on

3 onions, peeled and quartered

Makes 6 to 12 Servings

Time: A little over 2 hours

Season the cavity of bird with salt, thyme, and bay leaf. Place the peppercorns, cloves, large onions, celery, white wine, and capon in a large pot; add water to cover and a tablespoon of salt. Bring to a boil over medium-high heat. Lower the heat to a simmer and cook until the bird is just barely done, about 1½ hours. Gently remove the capon from the liquid.

Add the cabbage. Simmer for 10 minutes, then add the leek, the capon, and any accumulated cooking liquid. Cook 5 minutes, then add the potatoes, carrots, and onions. Cook another 10 minutes or until all the vegetables are tender but not mushy.

Remove the capon and the vegetables to a warm platter (if you like, cover the platter with foil and place it in a low temperature oven while you eat hors d'oeuvres or a first course). Carve the bird. Strain the broth. Pass the capon meat and vegetables, serving each guest a bowl of broth on the side.

Other greens to use:

Savoy or red cabbage.

○ ○ ○ ○ ○ ○ ○

This little twist on the traditional pot-au-feu is based on a brainstorm by my friend Jean-Louis Gerin, chef and owner of the eponymous restaurant in Greenwich, Conn. The broth is best served separately, before, or along with the vegetables and meat.

○ ○ ○ ○ ○ ○ ○

Oven-braised Pheasant with Sauerkraut

2 pheasant, about 2 pounds
  each
4 slices good bacon, diced
  (or substitute 3 tablespoons
  olive oil)
2 pounds sauerkraut
2 cloves
1 teaspoon juniper berries

½ teaspoon dried thyme, or
  one sprig fresh thyme
1 bay leaf
1 cup white wine
Stock or water as needed
Salt and pepper to taste

Makes 4 servings

Time: About 2½ hours, mostly unattended

To separate the birds' legs and breasts, cut through the skin that holds each leg to the body. Then use one hand to hold the bird by the back and the other to lift up on the breast until it is held only by a hinge on the back; sever the hinge. Set aside the breast and cut the legs and back into serving pieces.

In a large ovenproof skillet, sauté the bacon until crisp (or heat the olive oil until it shimmers). Add the leg pieces and brown on all sides. While they are browning, rinse the sauerkraut in a colander and preheat the oven to 300°F.

When the legs are nicely browned, add the sauerkraut, cloves, juniper berries, thyme, bay leaf, and white wine to the skillet. Sauté over medium heat until about half of the liquid has evaporated; move the skillet into the oven.

Bake for about 2 hours, stirring occasionally and adding liquid as needed, until the legs are tender and the sauerkraut very flavorful and slightly browned (don't worry about overcooking). Remove the skillet from the oven, discard the back pieces, check for seasoning, and cover to keep warm. Raise the oven temperature to 425°F. Salt and pepper the breasts and place them on a rack in a baking pan. Roast them for approximately 15 to 20 minutes; they should remain juicy and slightly pink.

Remove the breasts from the oven and put the skillet back in to reheat briefly. Slice the meat off the breasts, lay it over the leg pieces and sauerkraut, and serve.

○ ○ ○ ○ ○ ○ ○

This cooking technique makes best use of both legs and breasts of pheasant, and the simple presentation is quite elegant. Steer clear of canned sauerkraut, and look for a brand that contains no more than cabbage, salt, and water (health food stores usually have high-quality sauerkraut). This preparation also works well with chicken.

○ ○ ○ ○ ○ ○ ○

Grilled Chicken Breasts on Dandelion Greens

1 pound dandelion greens, washed and trimmed according to the directions on pages 6-8
1 pound boneless chicken breasts, sliced into cutlets
1 tablespoon olive oil

2 tablespoons honey
1 tablespoon dry sherry
1 tablespoon ground cumin
1 clove garlic, minced
Salt and pepper to taste
The juice of 1 lemon

Makes 4 servings
Time: About 20 minutes, plus time to preheat a grill

Steam the dandelion greens, covered, in a tiny bit of water just until wilted (page 8). Set aside to cool.

Start a charcoal or wood fire or preheat a gas grill or broiler; brush the chicken with the olive oil. Mix together the honey, sherry, cumin, garlic, and salt and pepper. Grill or broil the chicken 3 to 4 minutes per side, brushing once or twice with the honey-cumin mixture.

Meanwhile, squeeze the excess water from the greens, chop, mix with the lemon juice, salt, and pepper, and spread on a platter. Top with the chicken breasts when they are done.

○ ○ ○ ○ ○ ○ ○

This traditional Spanish combination of cumin and honey is delicious and a tad exotic. The cool, bitter, lemony greens contrast to add complexity to the dish.

○ ○ ○ ○ ○ ○ ○

Other greens to use:

Because of the sweetness of the chicken, this dish is best for bitter greens; use mustard, broccoli raab, turnips.

Stew of White Beans, Butternut Squash, and Kale

1 pound dried white beans
(cannelini, pea, Great
Northern, or navy), soaked
overnight

6 tablespoons olive oil

1 bay leaf

1 whole head garlic

1 large onion, diced

4 cloves garlic, peeled and
thinly sliced

1 tablespoon minced fresh
sage, or 1 teaspoon dried

1 teaspoon ground cumin

Pinch crushed red pepper
flakes

1 large butternut squash,
peeled, seeds removed, and
cut into 2-inch cubes

3 cups chicken stock or water,
more or less

Salt and pepper to taste

About one pound of kale,
washed and trimmed
according to the directions
on pages 6-8

Makes 6 servings

Time: 2 hours, with presoaked beans

In a large pot, add enough water to cover the beans plus 2 inches. Add 2 tablespoons olive oil, the bay leaf and garlic head. Simmer until the beans are tender, about 40 to 60 minutes. Drain, rinse with cold water, and drain again.

Remove the garlic (use it as a spread for bread or in other dishes). In a deep casserole, sauté the onion and slivered garlic in 2 tablespoons olive oil until translucent. Add the sage, cumin, and crushed red pepper and sauté 1 minute more. Add the squash and cook 1 minute, then add stock or water to cover.

Simmer for 15 minutes or until squash is just tender. Season with salt and pepper and stir in the beans. Keep warm while you prepare the kale. (The dish may be made several hours or even a day ahead up to this point.)

Tear or chop the kale coarsely. Add 2 tablespoons olive oil to a large skillet and heat until it shimmers. Add the kale, and without stirring, let it brown on the bottom as it becomes tender. It will wilt and become soft in 5 to 6 minutes.

To serve, place a portion of the stew on a plate and top with kale.

Other greens to use:

Broccoli raab.

○ ○ ○ ○ ○ ○ ○

A rich, filling, flavorful, and elegant dish based on one created by Peter Hoffman, chef and owner of Savoy, a wonderfully eclectic SoHo restaurant. It's at its most flavorful with rich chicken stock but is delicious made with water as well.

○ ○ ○ ○ ○ ○ ○

Crispy Skin Salmon with Gingery Kale

1 2-pound fillet of salmon, scaled

1 pound kale

5 tablespoons olive oil, approximately

1 teaspoon minced garlic

1 teaspoon grated ginger

1 tablespoon soy sauce

1 teaspoon dark sesame oil

Makes 4 servings

Time: 40 minutes

Rinse the fish well, remove any of the large "pin bones" that run down the center of the fillet (use a needle-nose pliers) and let it rest between paper towels, refrigerated, while you prepare the kale.

Wash the kale in several changes of water, and remove any pieces of stem thicker than $1/4$ inch in diameter. Steam in an inch of water until good and soft, 20 minutes or more. Drain, rinse in cool water, squeeze dry, and chop.

Preheat a covered gas grill or start a charcoal fire in a grill that can be covered. Heat 2 tablespoons of the olive oil in a 10-inch non-stick sauté pan. Add the garlic and sauté 1 minute; do not brown. Add the kale and cook, stirring occasionally for about 3 minutes; add the ginger and cook another minute, then add the soy sauce and sesame oil and turn off the heat. Remove to a platter and keep warm.

With a sharp knife, score the skin of the salmon in a cross-hatch pattern. Oil the fish well with the remaining olive oil. Put the fillet on the preheated grill, skin side down, and cover. Cook, undisturbed, 5 to 8 minutes, or until done. Remove carefully with a large spatula, and place atop the kale. Serve immediately, making sure everyone gets a piece of skin.

Other greens to use:

Broccoli raab, young collards, mustard, turnips.

◦ ◦ ◦ ◦ ◦ ◦ ◦

Gardeners beset by kale will love this dish, but so will everyone who appreciates the rich flavor of salmon, cut by sharp greens sparked with ginger. Steam the kale well in advance if it's more convenient for you.

◦ ◦ ◦ ◦ ◦ ◦ ◦

Sautéed Chicken Breast Steaks with Garlicky Kale

1 pound kale, washed and
  trimmed according to the
  directions on pages 6-8
5 tablespoons olive oil
Salt and pepper to taste
1 teaspoon minced garlic
1 clove garlic, peeled and
  crushed

2 whole boneless chicken
  breasts, about 1 to 1½
  pounds
Flour for dredging
1 egg, lightly beaten in a bowl
Bread crumbs for dredging
Minced parsley
2 lemons, cut into wedges

Makes 4 servings
Time: 40 minutes

Strip the kale leaves from the stems; parboil the stems (pages 8-9) until they are almost tender; then add the greens and cook another minute. Drain the kale; when it is cool enough to handle, chop it.

Heat about half the olive oil in a 10-or 12-inch non-stick skillet. Sauté the kale briskly until well mixed with the oil. Add the minced garlic and cook another 2 minutes, stirring. Remove the kale to a serving platter and keep warm.

Heat the remaining oil in the same skillet. Sauté the garlic clove while you prepare the chicken. Cut each breast in half, then dredge each half in the flour, dip in the egg, then dredge in bread crumbs. Sauté the chicken quickly, over medium-high to high heat, until lightly browned on both sides, seasoning as you cook; total cooking time should be about 6 minutes. Place the cooked chicken atop the greens and garnish with parsley. Serve with lemon wedges, squeezing fresh lemon juice atop the chicken and the greens.

Leftovers of this dish make great sandwiches.

Other greens to use:

Broccoli raab, young collards, mustard, turnips.

Spicy Pork with Spinach

1 pound pork tenderloin
About a pound of fresh
  spinach, washed according
  to the directions on page 39
2 tablespoons peanut oil
1½ tablespoons minced garlic
  (about 4 or 5 large cloves)

¼ teaspoon crushed red
  pepper flakes, or to taste
1 tablespoon soy sauce
Juice of ½ lime

Makes 4 servings
Time: About 15 minutes

Slice the pork as thinly as you can (it's easier if you freeze it for 15 to 30 minutes first). Cut the slices into bite-sized pieces. Chop or tear the spinach coarsely.

When you're ready to cook, have all ingredients ready—including a serving dish and rice if any. Mix together the pork and the spinach. Preheat a wok or a large sauté pan over high heat until it begins to smoke. Lower the heat to medium and add the peanut oil to the wok. Swirl it around and add the garlic. Stir once or twice. As soon as the garlic begins to color—about 15 seconds—return the heat to high and add the pork-spinach mixture. Stir quickly and add the red pepper. Stir frequently (but not constantly), just until meat loses its redness, a minute or two. Add soy sauce and lime juice, stir, turn off the heat, and serve over rice.

Other greens to use:

Almost anything tender and as bitter as you like. Try dandelions, arugula, cress, or mizuna.

⊙ ⊙ ⊙ ⊙ ⊙ ⊙ ⊙

In season, you can throw a handful of freshly chopped basil into this dish, adding it at the last minute. If you plan to cook this dish with rice, start the rice first; cooking this is the work of a moment.

⊙ ⊙ ⊙ ⊙ ⊙ ⊙ ⊙

Hamburgers with Spinach, Parsley, and Parmesan

1 pound (or 20 ounces, if
  you're buying packaged)
  spinach, washed according
  to the directions on page 39
1 cup minced parsley
1 pound freshly ground beef

¼ cup freshly grated
  Parmesan cheese
1 clove garlic, minced
Salt and pepper to taste

Makes 4 servings
Time: 30 minutes at most

Trim the spinach of the tips of its thickest stems, and steam it (page 8) with the water that clings to its leaves. When cool, squeeze out the water and chop finely.

Combine all ingredients gently and shape into burgers (or meatballs). Preheat a non-stick 12-inch skillet over medium-high heat for 3 or 4 minutes. Sprinkle the skillet with salt, raise the heat to high, and cook the burgers, gently, turning once, until nicely browned on both sides and done to medium-rare. Total cooking time will be about 6 to 8 minutes.

Other greens to use:

The slightly bitter tenderness of spinach makes it perfect here; chard is also good.

⊙ ⊙ ⊙ ⊙ ⊙ ⊙ ⊙

Time was that this recipe was what you'd call a method of "stretching" your meat. Now it's a fine recipe for minimizing the amount you eat while still enjoying its flavor. I like this best with ground sirloin, but you can use any cut you like.

⊙ ⊙ ⊙ ⊙ ⊙ ⊙ ⊙

Stir-fried Chicken with Broccoli Raab

1 boneless chicken breast,
  about 1 pound
1 tablespoon cornstarch
1 teaspoon minced ginger
1 teaspoon minced garlic
2 scallions, minced
1 tablespoon dry sherry
Salt to taste

About 1 pound broccoli raab,
  washed and trimmed
  according to the directions
  on pages 6-8
2 tablespoons peanut oil
1/2 cup stock or water
1 tablespoon soy sauce
1 teaspoon dark sesame oil

Makes 4 servings
Time: About 20 minutes

Cut the chicken into 1/2-inch chunks; mix with the cornstarch, ginger, garlic, scallions, sherry, and salt. Cut off the tough ends of the broccoli raab; if the stems are thicker than a pencil, use a paring knife to peel away the tough coating. Cut it into 1-inch pieces. Parboil (pages 8-9) until nearly tender, 3 to 5 minutes. Drain.

Heat a wok or large skillet over very high heat until smoking. Add 1 tablespoon of oil and the chicken mixture. Stir over high heat, about 2 minutes. Remove with a slotted spoon.

Add the remaining oil and the broccoli raab and stir-fry for 1 minute. Add the chicken stock, and cover and simmer for a minute or two. Return the chicken to the wok, stir, add soy sauce and optional sesame oil, and serve, with white rice.

You can, of course, stir-fry boneless chicken (or pork, tofu, or whatever) with any dark green; varying cooking times as needed.

Variation

Stir-fried Tofu with Cabbage: Use 1 cake firm tofu, cut into cubes of any manageable size you like; 1 pound cabbage, shredded; 1 medium onion, sliced. Omit cornstarch. Do not marinate; stir-fry ginger, garlic, scallions, onions, and cabbage together until tender, about 8 to 10 minutes; add sherry and remove from wok. Add remaining oil, tofu, and stock; cover and simmer 1 minute. Add soy sauce and cabbage mixture, sprinkle with sesame oil, and serve.

Other greens to use:

As noted above, almost any cooking green can be stir-fried successfully. Those with tougher stems such as collards and kale will need to be parboiled; more tender ones like dandelion and spinach can be cooked directly in the oil.

Fried Pork Salad with Cabbage and Avocados

1/4 cup crushed cumin seeds

3 tablespoons chili powder

1 tablespoon salt

1 tablespoon freshly cracked black pepper

1 pound boneless pork loin

1/4 cup olive oil

1 2-pound head green cabbage, cored and thinly sliced

1/2 cup lime juice (about 4 limes)

2 tablespoons minced fresh red or green chile pepper

1 red onion, finely diced

1 tablespoon minced garlic

2 ripe avocados, peeled, pitted, and cut into bite-sized chunks

1 cup freshly squeezed orange juice (about 2 oranges)

1/4 cup red wine vinegar

1/2 cup chopped fresh cilantro

1/4 cup pumpkin seeds, toasted in a sauté pan over medium heat until they begin to pop

Salt and freshly ground black pepper

Makes 6 servings

Time: About 30 minutes

In a small bowl, combine the cumin, chili powder, salt, and pepper; mix well. Slice the pork into 1/2-inch thick rounds and rub it well with this mixture.

In a large sauté pan, heat the olive oil until hot but not smoking. Put the pork in the skillet and cook over medium-high heat until nicely browned, 3 to 4 minutes per side. Remove and cut into thin slices.

In a large bowl, combine all the remaining ingredients and toss well. Lay the pork strips over the top of the salad and serve.

Other greens to use:

Red or Savoy cabbage.

⊚ ⊚ ⊚ ⊚ ⊚ ⊚ ⊚

A typically wild and wonderful dish created by my friends Chris Schlesinger and John Willoughby, authors of Thrill of the Grill *and* Born Under a Hot Sun.

⊚ ⊚ ⊚ ⊚ ⊚ ⊚ ⊚

"Sour" Chicken in a Pot with Cabbage

1 free-range or Kosher chicken, about 3 pounds

6 cups stock or water

3 onions, peeled and quartered

2 carrots, peeled and cut into chunks

1 bay leaf

Several allspice berries

Several peppercorns

Several sprigs of fresh thyme, or 1 teaspoon dried thyme

Salt and freshly ground black pepper

1 small cabbage, about a pound, cored and roughly chopped

1 cup cream, optional

1 egg, lightly beaten, optional

2 tablespoons top-quality wine vinegar

Makes 4 servings

Time: About an hour and a half

Rinse the chicken and put it in a pot with the stock or water, onions, and carrots. Bring to a boil and skim if necessary. Tie the bay leaf, allspice, peppercorns, and thyme sprigs, if any, in a small cheesecloth bag and add this to the pot along with the salt and pepper. Simmer about 45 minutes, until the chicken and vegetables are nearly tender; add the cabbage and cook until it is tender, another 15 minutes or so.

If you like, beat the cream and egg with the vinegar; add a cup of the hot stock to the mixture, stir, add this mixture to the pot, and heat through (do not boil). If you choose to omit the egg and cream, simply add the vinegar to the pot before serving.

Other greens to use:

Napa or Savoy cabbage.

Pasta with Broccoli Raab and Chicken

About 1½ pounds broccoli
  raab, washed and trimmed
  according to the directions
  on pages 6-8
2 tablespoons olive oil
1 teaspoon minced garlic
½ pound boneless chicken
  breast, trimmed and diced

2 cups canned plum tomatoes,
  drained and crushed
Salt and freshly ground
  black pepper
1 pound large pasta,
  such as penne
¼ cup minced fresh basil,
  parsley, or scallions

Makes 4 servings

Time: About 30 minutes

Bring a large pot of water to a boil, salt it liberally; chop the broccoli raab coarsely and cook it in the water until it is barely tender. Remove it with a slotted spoon and cool. Reserve the water.

Meanwhile, heat the olive oil over medium heat in a 10-inch skillet and add the garlic; cook just until the garlic colors, a minute or so, and add the chicken. Raise the heat to medium high and cook, stirring, until the chicken begins to brown a bit. Add the tomatoes and season to taste. Cook, stirring, over medium heat, until the tomatoes begin to break up.

Coarsely chop the broccoli raab and add it to the tomato sauce. Cook the pasta in the water you used for the broccoli, until tender but not mushy. Drain it and toss with the sauce, topping the dish with basil, parsley, or scallions.

This makes a fine, quick one-dish meal.

Other greens to use:

Collards, kale, or mustard.

Chicken Baked in Savoy Cabbage

12 large leaves from
Savoy cabbage
Salt and freshly ground
black pepper
1 pound boneless chicken
breast, cut into 12 thin slices
6 thick slices of tomato,
cut in half

3 tablespoons olive oil
Juice of a lemon
1/2 cup minced parsley
1 cup stock, or 1/2 cup water
mixed with 1/2 cup dry white
wine, approximately

Makes 4 servings
Time: About an hour

Bring a large pot of water to a boil; salt it. Preheat the oven to 400°F. Simmer the cabbage leaves, 1 or 2 at a time until tender, 15 to 30 seconds. Remove and rinse gently under cold water; drain.

Lay a leaf on a flat surface and top it with a piece of chicken, a slice of tomato, and a bit of olive oil, lemon juice, parsley, and salt and pepper. Roll it up, tucking the ends under to make a nice little package. Repeat the process until done.

Lay the packages next to each other, preferably in a baking pan that is just large enough to accommodate all of them. Add enough stock to come about halfway up the sides of the packages and bake, uncovered, until a thin-bladed knife can pierce the chicken quite easily, about 20 to 30 minutes. Serve, spooning a little of the cooking liquid over each package.

Variations

With Potato and Basil: Peel 1 large potato and slice it thinly; layer it between the chicken and tomato. Use vinegar instead of lemon juice, and top the mixture with a basil leaf before rolling. Omit parsley.

With Carrots and Zucchini: Use a bed of julienned carrots and zucchini, sprinkled with a few drops of vinegar; top with olive oil, tarragon, and a thin slice of lemon.

Other greens to use:

Anything big: Collards or kale (trim the thick stems), grape leaves (trim the veins), or white cabbage.

Corned Beef and Cabbage

A 3- to 5-pound corned beef
1 whole head garlic
2 onions, whole
10 peppercorns
5 allspice berries
2 bay leaves

5 cloves
2-pound cabbage, or larger,
  cored and cut into wedges
8 medium potatoes, peeled
  and cut in half

Makes 8 servings

Time: At least 2 hours

Place the meat in a large pot, cover it with water, and bring to a boil. Add the garlic and onions; tie the peppercorns, allspice, bay leaves, and cloves in small piece of cheesecloth (or use a tea ball or similar utensil). Simmer until the corned beef is quite tender (a thin-bladed knife will pierce it without much effort), about 2 hours. Add the cabbage and potatoes and cook until they are tender but not soggy, another 20 or 30 minutes. Turn off the heat, fish out the garlic, onion, and spices, and serve; this will hold in its liquid quite well for 30 minutes or so.

Other greens to use:

You want to mess with tradition? Try Savoy or Napa cabbage; to go really far afield, you can use Belgian endive or radicchio, but be careful not to overcook them.

Lamb Stew with Cabbage

1½ pounds boneless lamb, or 3 pounds bone-in, taken from the neck or shoulder

1 tablespoon olive or vegetable oil

1 large onion, peeled and sliced

3 cloves garlic, peeled and crushed

2 carrots, peeled and cut into chunks

1 cabbage, 1 to ½ pounds, cored and shredded

2 tablespoons flour

Salt and freshly ground black pepper

1 cup sturdy red wine

2 cups stock or water

½ cup minced parsley for garnish

Makes 4 servings

Time: At least an hour and a half

Trim the lamb of fat and cut into manageable pieces. Heat the oil over medium-high heat in a Dutch oven or casserole. Brown the meat well on all sides; remove it from the pan, reduce the heat to medium, and add the onion, garlic, and carrot. Cook, stirring occasionally until the onion wilts.

Add the cabbage and continue to cook and stir until the cabbage begins to wilt. Sprinkle with the flour, salt and pepper; stir; and add the wine. Let it bubble away for a minute or two, then add the stock or water. Cover and cook over low heat, stirring occasionally until tender, 1 to 2 hours depending on the cut. Remove the cover, boil away any excess liquid, garnish, and serve.

Variations

Lamb Stew with Cabbage, Tomatoes, and Red Pepper: Begin as in original recipe; after adding the cabbage, stir in 2 cups canned tomatoes, drained and chopped, and crushed red pepper or minced jalapeños (or other fresh hot peppers) to taste. Proceed as in original recipe.

Pork Stew with Cabbage: Follow original recipe, substituting pork for lamb and adding 4 peeled, quartered potatoes with the cabbage. Use white wine in place of red.

Other greens to use:

Napa, red, or Savoy cabbage.

Mixed Grill with Broccoli Raab

4 waxy potatoes

About 1½ pounds broccoli raab, washed and trimmed according to the directions on pages 6-8

½ pound garlicky sausage, such as chorizo, linguica, or Italian sausage

½ pound good bacon, preferably cut into thick slices

1 teaspoon minced garlic

1 tablespoon top-quality wine vinegar

Salt and freshly ground black pepper

Makes 4 servings

Time: About 40 minutes

Bring a medium-sized pot of water to a boil; peel the potatoes and cut them in half; salt the water and cook the potatoes until they are just tender. Remove the potatoes. In the same water, parboil (pages 8-9) the broccoli raab for about 3 minutes until it is bright green and beginning to become tender. Drain and run it under cold water for a few moments.

Meanwhile, heat a 12-inch non-stick skillet over medium-high heat for 3 to 4 minutes; put the sausage in the pan, prick it with a fork or thin-bladed knife a few times, and cook it, turning from time to time, until it is nicely browned. Remove it, add the bacon, and cook it carefully until crisp but not burnt. Remove the bacon with a slotted spoon, pour off excess fat, and brown the potatoes in the fat that remains.

Squeeze the excess liquid from the broccoli raab and chop it coarsely. Add it to the potatoes and cook, stirring occasionally, for 3 or 4 minutes. Cut the sausage and bacon into pieces and return them to the pan along with the garlic; reheat, add the vinegar, correct seasoning, and serve.

Other greens to use:

Collards, kale, mustard.

Braised Sauerkraut with Ham Hocks and Apples

2 tablespoons lard or lightly
flavored oil

1 large or 2 medium onions,
peeled and sliced

2 tart, crisp apples, such as
Granny Smith, Empire, or
Golden Delicious, peeled,
cored, and thinly sliced

1½ pounds sauerkraut

1 bay leaf

1 teaspoon juniper berries

½ cup gewurtraminer or
riesling, not too dry

1 cup stock or water

2 ham hocks

Makes 4 servings

Time: About an hour

Heat the lard or oil over medium heat until hot, and add the onion and apple; toss until the onion begins to wilt. Lower the heat to medium, add the sauerkraut, and stir; add the bay leaf, juniper berries, and the wine and stir; cook a minute or 2 until some of the wine bubbles away. Bury the ham hocks in the sauerkraut, add the stock or water, cover, lower the heat, and cook until the sauerkraut and meat are tender, about 30 minutes. Remove the bay leaf and serve immediately.

◎ ◎ ◎ ◎ ◎ ◎

This is very similar to Sauerkraut Braised in Wine (page 127), but is an extremely hearty main course.

◎ ◎ ◎ ◎ ◎ ◎ ◎

Stir-fried Monkfish with Napa Cabbage and Red Peppers

¾ to one pound
  monkfish fillets
1 tablespoon rice or
  white vinegar
¼ cup peanut or vegetable oil
1 teaspoon minced garlic
1 teaspoon minced peeled
  ginger
2 scallions, minced

1 red bell pepper, seeds
  removed, cut into strips
2 cups shredded
  Napa cabbage
Salt and freshly ground
  black pepper
½ cup stock or water
1 tablespoon soy sauce

Makes 4 servings
Time: 30 minutes

Preheat a wok over high heat. Cut the monkfish into 1-inch chunks. Toss with the vinegar and set aside. Add the oil to the wok, and then immediately add the garlic, ginger, and scallions. Stir-fry for 30 seconds, then add the pepper slices. Cook one minute and add the cabbage. Add salt and pepper; if you feel that the cabbage is cooking too slowly, cover the wok. If not, toss and cook for about 5 minutes. Add the stock, soy sauce, and monkfish, and cook about 3 minutes, until the fish is done. Serve immediately, with rice.

Other greens to use:

Red or white cabbage.

◦ ◦ ◦ ◦ ◦ ◦

Monkfish fillets are perfect for stir-frying. The pieces are done in a couple of minutes and they will not fall apart. You can make this dish with boneless chicken breasts or tofu if you like.

◦ ◦ ◦ ◦ ◦ ◦

A Note to the Gardener

EVERYONE who has a bit of dirt should grow greens. You can start them earlier in the year than anything else—I'm out there the instant the ground thaws—and you can harvest them later. (If the weather holds for four more days, we'll be eating our kale, fresh from the ground, on Christmas Day.) If you live in more temperate climes than New England, you can grow greens right through the winter.

Greens attract fewer pests than fruiting vegetables and are stricken by fewer diseases. They are prolific, and are not heavy feeders. They're easy to grow, even organically. Do you need more reasons? The seeds are cheap, the varieties endless, the plants themselves attractive. Go plant some.

When you're ready to order, here are my favorite sources, with comments (you can also buy seeds for greens from standard gardening catalogues, such as Burpee and Parks):

Nichols Garden Nursery, 1190 North Pacific Highway, Albany, OR 97321. (503) 928-9280. The best selection, great prices, and very friendly people. Planting instructions and information supplied by the catalogue is minimal, but where else are you going to find edible chysanthemums? I buy 80 percent of my seeds from Nichols.

Shepherd's Garden Seeds, 30 Irene St., Torrington, CT 06790. (203) 482-3638. Shepherd's has a small selection, and it is expensive, but the quality is unsurpassed. Wonderful, carefully selected varieties, first-rate seed.

J. L. Hudson, Seedsman, Box 1058, Redwood City, CA 94064. Quirky, near-brilliant catalogue, mostly flowers. But a few choice items for those who are looking for esoterica.

Territorial Seed Company, 20 Palmer Avenue, Cottage Grove, OR 97424. (503) 942-9881. I have not ordered from this catalogue, but intend to do so this year. Its selection of Asian greens rivals that of Nichols.

index

Tofu, stir-fried with cabbage, 176
Tortellini and Chard in Broth, 64
Tumbleweed, 14
Tuna steaks, grilled with mesclun stuffing, 162
Turnip greens, 41
  in Mustard Sauce, 123
  with Potatoes, 110
  and Scallops Soup, 54

U

Upland cress, 42

V

Vinaigrette
  Anchovy-Caper, 99
  Basic, 95
  Creamy, 96
  Lemon, 97
  Lime, 98
  Mayonnaise Style, 100
  Nutty, 99
  Orange, 98
  Walnut Oil, 96
Vitamins, greens and, 4

W

Wakame and Cucumber Salad, 72; *see also* Sea vegetables
Walnut Oil Vinaigrette, 96
Warm Salad of Mâche
  and Beets, 88
  and Scallops, 88
Wasabe Swordfish with Spinach and Soy, 161
Washing greens, 6–7

Water soluble nutrients, cooking and, 5
Watercress, 42
  and Sesame Salad, 81
  Soup, 65
    with Potatoes, 65
White
  chard, 40
  mustard, 31–32
Whole Croutons, 91
Wild greens, 42–43
Willoughby, John, 80
Winter purslane, 33–34
Witloof, 16

Z

Zinc, 4